"*Finding God in the Bible* is real and gut-level honest, filled with the things necessary to inspire a person to follow Jesus at any cost. This book is the essence of authentic. Darren lives in the pursuit of answers. But the backstory of this book is that where no immediate answers are available, there is a relationship with God that is more than enough."

> from the foreword by Bill Johnson, senior leader, Bethel Church, Redding, California; author, *When Heaven Invades Earth*, *Hosting the Presence* and many more

"Darren is a master storyteller who takes us on a journey to discover what friendship with God can really be like. He highlights one of my favorite themes when he emphasizes how God honors our relationship with Him more than our service for Him. *Finding God in the Bible* is sure to stir up fresh hunger for God's Word and lead you into deeper intimacy with the One who longs to know you more. As you dive in, I pray that you will feast at the table with the One who humbles Himself and calls us friend."

> Heidi Baker, Ph.D., founding director of Iris Global

"Darren Wilson is one of the most innovative filmmakers and authors of faith today. With his latest book, he takes you on a discovery of God like no one else before. *Finding God in the Bible* will blow you away!"

> DeVon Franklin, senior vice president, Columbia TriStar Pictures

"I love Darren's ability to deal with the Bibles paradoxes and yet lead the reader out of confusion into conviction. *Finding God in the Bible* gives the reader permission to trust God without having it all figured out. As you read this book, you will experience the reality that friendship is possible with the Invisible One."

Bryan Schwartz, pastor, Renovation Church, Denver; former NFL linebacker

FINDING GOD

IN THE BIBLE

FINDING GOD

GOD

IN THE BIBLE

WHAT CRAZY PROPHETS,
FICKLE FOLLOWERS AND DANGEROUS OUTLAWS
REVEAL ABOUT FRIENDSHIP WITH GOD

DARREN WILSON

Chosen

a division of Baker Publishing Group
Minneapolis, Minnesota

© 2013 by Darren Wilson

Published by Chosen Books
11400 Hampshire Avenue South
Bloomington, Minnesota 55438
www.chosenbooks.com

Chosen Books is a division of
Baker Publishing Group, Grand Rapids, Michigan

Printed in the United States of America

Library of Congress Cataloging-in-Publication Data
Wilson, Darren.
    Finding God in the Bible : what crazy prophets, fickle follwers and danger-
ous outlaws reveal about friendship with God / Darren Wilson.
        p.   cm.
    Summary: "A fresh, eye-opening, and sometimes humorous look at the sto-
ries and characters in the Bible and how they all reveal an even bigger picture of
our loving Father"—Provided by publisher.
    ISBN 978-0-8007-9558-0 (pbk. : alk. paper)
    1. God—Biblical teaching. I. Title.
BS544.W55 2013
220.6—dc23   2013010812

Cover design by Gearbox

13   14   15   16   17   18   19   7   6   5   4   3   2   1

I dedicate this book to my children: Serenity, Stryder and River. You three more than anyone have taught me the profound nature of a father's love for his children. If I, being a selfish and flawed man, can love you with such depth and want only what is best for you, I simply cannot comprehend how much more our Father loves us unconditionally and desires good and perfect things for us. Thank you for teaching me about the Father's heart, and thank you for being three terrific kids. I love you and am so very proud of you.

Contents

Foreword

I have been both spectator and participant in the unfolding journey of Darren Wilson. I have seen the sovereign work of God as He selected this man—someone who had seemingly little-to-no interest in spiritual matters. And I've also seen what has become a growing hunger that drives this man beyond himself to engage God in a way that confronts all fears. His is truly a remarkable story, one that must be told. God took a complacent college professor and turned him into one of the spark plugs for a worldwide move of God.

Finding God in the Bible comes along at a time when a generation is crying out for a Gospel that will make sense of things in a way that stained-glass windows and Christian routine have not. This cry has opened a door to many messages that carry the name of Jesus, but are not the Gospel at all. They tickle the ears but contain little transformational power. Thankfully, *Finding God in the Bible* is not that way at all. It is real and gut-level honest, yet it is filled with the things necessary to inspire a person to follow Jesus at any cost. This book is the essence of authentic.

On these pages, you will find great and sometimes humorous perspectives into difficult passages of Scripture. It also contains a roadmap of someone who came alive at Jesus' invitation: "Follow Me." This book provides a perfect blend of inspiration and insight.

Darren asks questions that many ignore. He then gives answers, but not as a "know-it-all." He answers as a man on a journey, a journey of growing friendship with God. One of the great tragedies in Christianity is to have the Bible interpreted by people who are not in love. Darren presents the antidote to that issue by speaking out of the core of his being—his identity as a friend of God. I have no doubt that Darren would have considered himself the least qualified for "friendship with God." Perhaps that's what qualified him most.

For a long time, the Church has tolerated a strange form of dishonesty. It's called "hype." It grieves me to see the Church create a culture in which hype is normal. Hype creates expectations it cannot fulfill. Living with theories and disappointment becomes the norm in that environment. Thus, a generation sits in that condition week after week until finally they choose something that is lesser, but will at least be honest. The raw but honest nature of Darren's books and films speaks more than adequately to this issue. The timing couldn't be more perfect or important.

Darren lives in the pursuit of answers. But the backstory of this book is that where no immediate answers are available, there is a relationship with God that is more than enough.

This posture allows for the peace that passes understanding to guard us and keep us safe in a hostile environment. In other words, the peace of His presence will suffice until we gain insight for our God-inspired quest for understanding. Such faith was at the heart of the issue for all our heroes of Scripture and Church history.

When individuals deal with the matters of the heart, they are making history with God. When they make history with God, they become positioned for God to make history through them. That is the case for Darren Wilson. He has said yes to God on every level. And now his writings and films are both making history and marking history.

I commend to you *Finding God in the Bible*. I also commend to you his films: *Finger of God*, *Furious Love* and *Father of Lights*. They are all life-changing in the fullest sense of the word. And, finally, I commend to you the man Darren Wilson, a personal friend, and, more importantly, a friend of God.

Bill Johnson, senior leader,
Bethel Church, Redding, California

1

The God of the Bible: My BFF

In case you weren't aware, God is an author. He wrote a book. Not only that, His book is a bestseller. In fact, the Bible is on record as the all-time bestseller in publishing history. If you haven't read it, you should check it out. It has everything you need in a good story: action, adventure, romance, intrigue, betrayal, death, rebirth, the salvation of the whole world—His book is seriously epic. It's so good, in fact, that God never felt the need to write a sequel. His one and only book is pure perfection.

Being an author and professional storyteller myself (although slightly less successful than God), I see His book through a lens that's different from a lot of other people's lenses. While it is certainly the Word of God—and I stake my entire life on what is written on those pages—still, I cannot separate myself from the fact that it is also . . . well . . . a book.

While countless others have ruminated on the meanings of the stories, concepts and applications of His book, I want to take a look at it from a slightly different perspective. I want to understand more about the Author based on His decisions and actions within the book. Let me explain what I mean.

As every storyteller will confirm, countless hours go into a composition to make sure that it is accurate and entertaining. But beyond that, we also work hard on every nuance to make sure that the story says exactly what we want it to say. This is because a story reveals as much about its author as it does about the characters created within. I always tell my students that they can't hide their true selves from me: All I need to do is read their stories.

I believe that all stories carry various levels of this "author-stamping," as I call it. Every story I write, for instance, no matter what it is about, will always wind up being about redemption. That is because this is what means the most to me in life. Along the way, I might write about things that push the boundaries of what some Christians deem "acceptable." I am not afraid to write a swear word, for instance. Nor am I afraid to paint a realistic picture of a terrible act, even if it might upset someone.

This is a reflection of my upbringing more than anything else. I was raised in the home of an artist and taught from a very young age that the status quo is not something I am to strive for. Great art meets people and moves people right where they are. When I write something, I want to explore the tensions of faith and the human experience. My work as a storyteller involves careful crafting, certainly, but it is also both an artistic decision and a window into my soul.

It is my contention, then, that God, who is the greatest artist of all time, reveals much of Himself in His story. And since He is such a complete artist, I could spend my lifetime searching His book and continue to come up with new revelations of His character hidden inside. The fact is, God basically begs us to pick apart His book in this way, as He not only writes about a wide variety of characters, lowlifes and outlaws, but actually goes so far as *to enter His own story physically.* Only God could dare do such a thing.

Everything we will study here hangs on that assumption— that God is revealing His own character through His interaction with the characters He has created, and what He chose to write about that interaction.

I think, for instance, it's a fairly safe assumption that God had more interaction and conversations with Moses than are recorded in the Bible. One can only conclude that He had a good reason for what He kept and what He cut.

Or what about Enoch? I think that Enoch is one of the top five most fascinating characters in the Bible, and God basically gives us *a couple of sentences* about the guy! "Enoch walked with God three hundred years, and then he was no more because God took him away." That's it? Enoch is one dude I will be making a beeline for as soon as I get to heaven. I guarantee you that he has some stories that will make your hair stand on end. But why doesn't God tell any of them to us? Anyone who walks with God for three hundred years with that kind of intimacy has to have seen some wild stuff. The only other person in the Bible to get that kind of an exit is Elijah, and next to Jesus, he takes the cake for wacky miraculous encounters.

So why is God silent on Enoch? You might have different interpretations of many of the things we discuss in this book—which is what makes God that much greater a storyteller!—but in the case of Enoch, I wonder if maybe God is showing us that sometimes He wants things to be just between us and Him.

If God has shown us anything, it's that He is a God who yearns to be intimate with us. That is the whole reason He sent His Son here. He wants a relationship with us, but we are such idiots, so dirty and sinful, that in order for that to happen, someone had to pay for our idiocy. That He sent His own Son to do it reveals much of His character.

The Best Laid Plans

I first discovered this aspect of intimacy in God's character at a moment when I felt like a total creative failure.

I make movies for a living. It just so happens that those movies are about God. This was not something I chose to do exactly. When I was a kid, I didn't stare out the window and fantasize about someday changing the world through movies designed to capture the essence of an invisible God. Being a filmmaker was never a dream of mine, even when I went to film school. I wanted to *write* movies, not make them.

I remember taking aptitude tests when I was in grade school. They were supposed to identify what you were "geared for," what kind of a career you were most likely to enter into when you were a grown-up. I remember how nervous I was the first time I took one of those things. It was like filling out an application to have your fortune told. It seemed kind of heavy for a ten-year-old kid. What was it going to tell me? What if I didn't like what it said? My little kid brain could not grasp the notion of personality profiles. All I knew was that this thing was going to tell me what I was going to be when I grew up. I secretly hoped it would come back as "the next Michael Jordan."

That didn't happen. Nonetheless, I breathed a sigh of relief when I saw the results. Even as a kid, it seems, I had an aptitude for writing and teaching. That's what the test revealed anyway. I thought, *Yeah, I can do that. Anything other than manual labor sounds good to me.* I grew up in Monroe, Michigan, a blue-collar, pseudo-farm town, and most of my friend's dads worked up at the Ford plant near Detroit. That was always my worst nightmare: working at the plant. Not because I hated cars, but because I knew that I was built to write stories.

At first I was sure I would be a famous author. Then I was determined to be a successful screenwriter (because there is really no such thing as a famous screenwriter). But never did filmmaker, director or movie producer enter my head. Not once did I dabble in home movies. I liked movies, but simply because I liked stories. As a teenager I read the classics. For fun! I was such a nerd.

But as we will see in this book, God always knows us better than we know ourselves. His genius astounds me every day. Somehow, He saw a public speaker in this quiet kid who couldn't talk without tripping over his words. He saw a filmmaker in a writer who had no interest (and still doesn't) in cameras. He saw a heart that would be wholly devoted to Him even when friendship with Him was the last thing I wanted.

The Most Unlikely One

So it was with a sense of career failure, on a cold December night in 2005, that I sat in my crummy townhouse just outside of Chicago, staring at the fading embers of a fire in my crumbling fireplace. It was a perfect metaphor for my life. My hopes for success as a writer were about as dead as they could be. The coals of ambition were not even hot anymore. I kept churning out stories because I enjoyed the process, but reality was settling in. As I neared thirty, my life was coming into focus. I had been a college professor since age 23, and that was all I was ever going to be. Not a bad gig, but not what I had always wanted. I had no more ideas left even to try. I was blocked. It was over. The smoke was rising from the ashes of my hopes and dreams.

I trudged upstairs to bed. My wife, Jenell, had gone up a while before. We had just fought, again, about something I thought was totally stupid. She wanted me to ask God for an idea to write about. She saw my blockage, saw a husband who could barely tolerate church anymore, and she had tried everything to jump-start my heart and passion for God. I had endured passive-aggressive conversations, shaming, strategically placed books around the house, open begging, silent treatments—the works, really. I told her the only thing that

20

ever really helped was when she left me alone and prayed for me, but that was always hard for her because it felt as though she was giving up.

I didn't want to do it . . . ask God for an idea. It felt like the ultimate end to a failed dream. I wasn't even sure I believed in God anymore. Well, not the God I grew up with. It all seemed so contrived. Church had become a subculture built to keep itself alive. I was overwhelmed by the fake smiles and the fake handshakes and the fake conversations. I wanted something real.

But then again, I didn't. I knew that if I ever got something real, I'd be responsible for it. If something is true and you find out about it, then action must follow. If God could really be the Friend that I had been hearing about from my family and my wife, who kept attending all these crazy charismatic conferences, then, man, that was seriously going to change things. And as much as I wanted to succeed creatively, I wanted that much more for my spiritual life to remain the same. I might have raged against the status quo in my creative life, but I fully embraced it spiritually. Why? Because it was safe.

By the time I got into bed, though, I was a defeated man. As I sank my head into my pillow, I prayed a shallow, unbelieving prayer.

"God, if You've got an idea, I guess I'll take it."

Like a bombshell, the idea exploded in my brain. My eyes flew open. I jumped out of bed and ran downstairs to write it down. The words that poured out formed the opening salvo for my first feature film.

Many of the events that happened next—from my encounter with an angel five months later to entering the world of film directing and production—are told in my book *Filming God*. I saw and heard things during those four years that not only ignited my cold, stale heart for God, but also drew me slowly, relentlessly, into newfound and wholly unexpected friendship with Him.

I started my first film, *Finger of God*, wondering if God would do anything at all when I turned on the camera. During my second film, *Furious Love*, I knew He would probably do stuff, and I started to believe that He would show up wherever I went. With my third film, *Father of Lights*, I knew He would back me up. By the time I reached the end of filming that movie (the wild Dome of the Rock sequence) I was asking things of Him and expecting things of Him that only a friend would. My journey from skeptic jerk to friend of God was complete.

In essence, this book is about friendship with God. All of the stories that we will explore here reflect His great desire to be intimate with us, His children. I believe that He wants to have a broad spectrum of relationships with us—Father, Lover, Mother, Teacher, Savior, Protector. But it is my contention that His chief aim, the reason He took such care in giving His marvelous book to us, is so that we might know Him, forever and ever, as our devoted, loving, trustworthy Friend.

You will not read here an exhaustive listing of things God has done. Rather you will find a smattering of examples from the Bible that I feel best reveal this aspect of His character. From Moses to Abraham to David to those wacky prophets, we have much to discover about Him by looking at the way He treats His friends.

I have written this book as much for myself as for anyone else. Having spent the last six years on a personal journey of discovery of the living God, and having met countless amazing people around the world who have had mind-boggling encounters with Him, I wanted to weigh all of these experiences against the Scriptures and try to see where God has revealed Himself as Friend throughout His story.

In the end, everything points to God. As Jesus said to the religious leaders who were trying to get Him to quiet the worshiping crowds, "Hey, if they don't do this, the flipping rocks will cry out!" Well, that's kind of what He said.

So let's start looking under some rocks, shall we?

2

Creation and Kisses

As a storyteller, I am acutely aware of the importance of a good beginning. If you don't start your story off with a bang, you are in big trouble because more than likely your audience is not going to have the patience to stick with you. There is also a level of trust implicit in all beginnings, a kind of nonverbal contract where you promise your readers that (1) you know what you're doing, and (2) you're about to take them on a fun ride.

If all great stories need to start off with a bang, God, as usual, shows all of us mere mortals how it's supposed to be done. Like a seasoned rocker who wants to show all the upstarts what real rock 'n' roll sounds like, He starts His story with the biggest bang imaginable. The Big Bang. Literally. He speaks and—*bang!*—the creation of the universe.

Scientists tell us that the universe is not only expanding, but doing so at an ever-increasing rate of speed. This is a testament to the fact that God's voice from the very beginning continues to echo through space and time. As for the increase in speed? I'm no physicist, but from the looks of things I think we can fairly safely conclude that when God gives a command, it not only gets the job done but also carries a little something called momentum. So don't be surprised when God works through you and it continues to grow bigger and more wonderful and sometimes faster than you ever dreamed. It's just God's momentum. He is like a steam locomotive picking up speed, and He is unstoppable. This aspect of His character is built into the very fabric of the universe.

So God decides to open His story with the creation of the world. Not a bad start. Now let's take a closer look at some of the "firsts" of His book. We'll find that they are both descriptive and revealing of His nature and character as Friend.

A Creative God

Here is the first line from God to humanity. It is the first thing He is going to reveal of Himself to the world, so we can assume that He puts a lot of thought into this, His introduction:

In the beginning God created the heavens and the earth.

Genesis 1:1

I find it fascinating that the first thing He decides to tell us about Himself is *not* that He is a God of love. Or covenant.

Or goodness. Or forgiveness. Or patience. Or grace. All of that is soon to come—and, in fact, the rest of His book takes great pains to show us those aspects of Himself in detail. But for some reason, the first thing God wants us to know about Him is that He is creative.

Created. It's the fifth word in the Bible, and the first word of any real substance (aside from God's name, of course). This is the opening shot from the storytelling bow. God takes aim at an aspect of Himself that is often overlooked on Sunday mornings: God is creative. In fact, God is creativity itself. Why does He start His book with this? The answer, I believe, goes to the heart of His hopes for us as individuals, as well as His collective Body.

As we will see throughout God's book, He is wildly creative in the ways He goes about His business. In the Person of Jesus, we see this creativity constantly in action. He's always taking people by surprise, always using creative stories to illustrate His point—and He rarely heals anyone the same way twice. One blind man gets spat upon; another is simply told he is healed.

Man often tries to take these creative acts and turn them into formulas for healing and ministry. I understand the concept: If this is the way Jesus did stuff, then how can you go wrong by copying the Master? (I'm still waiting to hear about a "spit ministry," though.) The problem is that if God is creativity incarnate, then by His very nature He cannot be placed into a formula. There is no five-step program to getting God to show up or listen to you. He is not a caged animal to be brought out by the beating of drums or the playing of flutes. He is a wild lion here, a meek and quiet lamb there.

He is an eagle one time, a gazelle the next. By showing us at the very start that He is creative, God is trying to tell us that He cannot be put in a box.

But of course, the Church has been trying to do just that for quite some time now.

A God in a box is much easier to deal with than one who is wild and unchained. We can understand a captive God, and, most importantly, we can *control* Him. But God cannot and will not be caged, controlled or boxed in. We can try all we want, but as soon as we do, God, in essence, hightails it out of there. He wants no part of captivity. So we continue with our rituals, with our formulaic Christianity, all the while thinking that God is pleased with us, that He is just loving the fact that we are the chosen ones who understand Him and are putting on such a fine show for Him. Unfortunately, we're usually the last ones to realize that God vacated the premises long ago.

When you remove the opportunity for God to be creative in the Church, you are left with religion. Religion in its most grotesque form is a system built upon principles, rules and empty theology; the heart has been ripped out. It's like zombie church. We are walking around, interacting with people, doing "churchy" things, but we are stiff and stale and not particularly pleasing. In fact, most people run from us when we're doing zombie church. Zombie churches don't attract people; they simply live to survive.

We know it is possible to "do church" without heart, as the church in Ephesus was told:

> "You have persevered and have patience, and have labored for My name's sake and have not become weary. Nevertheless I

have this against you, that you have left your first love. Remember therefore from where you have fallen."

Revelation 2:3–5

Here God is saying, in no uncertain terms, that no matter how good our intentions are, no matter how much we endure and how hard we work for the Kingdom, if we don't operate the way He wants us to operate (that is, abounding in love) then He is actually going to hold that against us!

Then, of course, we have the famous admonition to the church in Laodicea given in Revelation 3:14–22—which is the church most closely associated with the Western Church today. This is where God tells us that if we're lukewarm, He will spit us out of His mouth. You only spit stuff out that you don't want to be a part of you anymore. God doesn't sugarcoat it—if you try to peg Him as being this way and only this way, and if you're more interested in playing church than you are in Him and His kids, then He is going to have to move on from you (not personally, but corporately). You have probably heard of the term *dead church*. This (a church bent on activity over relationship) is one of the main reasons for that deadness. As the lead singer of U2, Bono, once said: "Religion is what's left when the Spirit leaves the building."

The Breath of God

Returning to our story, as God is creating the world, He does so by simply speaking things into existence. When God speaks, His words become law. Nothing in the universe can undo His words because the entire universe was created by His words, which makes it subject to His words. But when it comes time to create man, God takes a different approach:

> The LORD God formed man of the dust of the ground, and breathed into his nostrils the breath of life; and man became a living being.
>
> Genesis 2:7

Instead of simply saying, "Let there be man," which seems logical given His track record for creation up to this point, He now gets on His hands and knees and scoops up a pile of dirt and forms man as a potter would form clay. It is as if God is intentionally telling us that even amidst the glories of His universe, we are the thing He takes the most time with and are, therefore, His prized possessions.

What happens next, though, changes the whole game. As I just mentioned, up until now God is speaking things into existence. It would make sense, then, that after creating Adam, He would speak the word *Live* and Adam would begin breathing. Adam's body would have to obey God's command, and His heart would have to start beating, and his brain would have to start functioning. But God apparently has something else in mind for this creation of His. I think He also wants to show us His intentions right from the start.

Genesis tells us that God "breathed the breath of life" into Adam. In essence, He breathes part of Himself into us. And at this point, remember, the only thing we know about Him is that He is creative. This means that if you are breathing right now, you, too, are a creative being. Don't forget: This is one of the major things that separate us from the animals.

But even more profound than His breathing Himself into us is the fact that He chooses to breathe anything into us at all. Think about it: What is the only way you can breathe your breath into someone? Your lips must touch the other person's lips.

God's first act toward mankind is a kiss.

Lest there be any mistaking God's intentions toward us, lest we forget that the thing He desires above all else with us is relationship, we need only look at this first act. It is loaded with symbolism. If it isn't enough that He gets His hands dirty shaping us into existence, then the fact that He stoops to our level and places His pure, holy lips upon ours so that we might have something of Him inside of us, whether we believe in Him or not, is heartbreakingly beautiful.

But it doesn't stop there.

Ignition

Next we see God's first words to man. This is it: the moment of truth. I can just see Adam and Eve standing there, naked, holding hands as their Creator settles in to speak to them for the first time. The nervous energy crackling in the air—the aroma of God's love pouring over them. What is He going to say? What is He going to do?

> And God blessed them. And God said to them, "Be fruitful and multiply and fill the earth and subdue it."
>
> Genesis 1:28 ESV

The first sentence to man: *Be fruitful, multiply and subdue the earth*. On the surface, it may seem like a letdown. That's it? A weird, vague command? Yet, in reality, this statement is dripping with meaning.

God is far too good a storyteller to overlook even the tiniest detail. We can assume, therefore, that the order of His words carries a message as well. I don't think it is by random chance that He chooses to say "Be fruitful" first, followed by "multiply and subdue" next. I think God understands all too well the people He has just created. We would get the second and third parts of His first sentence quite well, thank you very much. Sex and power. We're on it, Captain. Those are orders we can happily follow.

But "be fruitful"? I think He says that first because it is dearest to His heart for us. While we as a race may care most about sex and power, He cares most about our fruitfulness, our sense of meaning in the world. He wants us to strive for excellence, to use our time well, to be intentional with our gifts—not so much for His and His Kingdom's sake, but for our sake! What we do on this earth means something to Him. It should, therefore, mean something to us as well.

But God has not finished teaching us through His interactions with Adam, not by a long shot, because what comes next takes that whole notion of fruitfulness and gives it an injection of righteous steroids.

Time to Go to Work

God has created man. He has breathed life into him, and that life carries the essence of His creativity. So it is only natural for God to want to take His new creation out for a test drive. Which brings about the first job given to man:

> Now the LORD God had formed out of the ground all the wild animals and all the birds in the sky. He brought them to the man to see what he would name them; and whatever the man called each living creature, that was its name.
>
> Genesis 2:19 NIV

Man's first assignment is a creative one: Give all the animals on earth names. God is showing all of us that we are not created primarily to plow the fields or build shelters or tend the flocks; nor are we even created primarily to do His bidding. We are free agents right from the start, and He hands us the wheel of His new creation and tells us to take it for a spin. He passes the creative buck of naming all the animals to us. This shows both God's immense humility as well as His trust in our abilities.

The implications here are profound. For one, our words carry weight with God. He pays attention to what we say and what we proclaim. It's why the Bible tells us that a man who can tame his tongue is perfect (see James 3:2). Our mouths are our biggest asset as well as our greatest enemy. We can bless or curse, and the reason for that is because God cares about what we say. He has given us an amazing and dangerous authority over His creation and each other (more on that later).

Even more telling is the implication that God feels joy and anticipation in letting Adam be creative. You can just see Him leaning forward, interest piqued, a smile spreading across His face as Adam takes a deep breath and dives in.

But it also implies something that should free us all in our quest for fruitfulness. God is showing here that He is interested in what Adam is about to do.

Which means that He derives pleasure from Adam's creative act.

Which means that He derives pleasure from our creative acts.

Which makes our creative acts . . . worship.

God Giggles?

Maybe it's the strange way my brain works, but to me, we come now to one of the coolest sentences in the Bible. I'm not sure how important it is in the grand scheme of things, but, then again, this book is about uncovering some of the smaller details peppered throughout the Bible that reveal aspects of God's character, and this one is a perfect example:

> They [the man and his wife] heard the sound of the LORD God walking in the garden in the cool of the day.
>
> Genesis 3:8

First, the obvious. Not until Jesus shows up on the scene will God again so openly and brazenly walk on the earth in our midst. Who knows if He still does it on His own, out in the wild somewhere, just for old time's sake? It's probably best for us not to conjecture too much on that and turn God into some kind of holy Sasquatch. Let's stay focused on what this says about God's character and the kind of relationship He desires with us.

We all know that the pre-Fall Garden of Eden was the way God *intended* for His creation to be. No death, apparently (meaning no steak—a serious flaw in the system if you ask me), and this curious little admission on God's part. He walked with Adam and Eve in the cool of the day. The God of the universe took human form and came down just to hang out with Adam and Eve. Who knows what kinds of conversations they had? Maybe He taught them biology. Or algebra. Or the way His world works. Maybe He had to explain the birds and the bees to them. Maybe He just listened to them. Maybe He told them jokes.

I have to stop here and tell you a story. If you have seen my film *Father of Lights*, you've met Ravi, whose friendship is one of the most unique gifts I've ever been given. He hears the audible voice of God every day. I mean it, audible. He wakes up and God tells him whom he's going to meet that day and what he's supposed to say to them. Sometimes He gives Ravi GPS turn-by-turn directions to head somewhere and save a lost or kidnapped child. Ravi has a million stories of crazy stuff God has asked him to do, but this particular story bears telling because it shows exactly why God gave Ravi this gift and not someone as simpleminded and moronic as me.

I was filming with Ravi in India for *Father of Lights*, and we were driving somewhere—I don't remember the particulars. Ravi is my friend, so I feel comfortable enough to ask him stupid questions all the time. I mean, how many people am I going to meet who have audible conversations with God every day? So, my mind going to its usual strange place, I asked him:

"Hey, Ravi, is God, like, super serious all the time?"

"Well, He's very funny, but when He's talking business, He's all business."

"Has He ever told you a joke?"

Ravi laughed. I'm pretty sure no one had ever asked him that before. "No, sir."

"You should ask God to tell you a joke."

Ravi laughed some more.

"I'm serious! Can you imagine what a joke from God would be like? It would have to be the funniest joke in the history of the world!"

Ravi continued laughing. Then he thought for a moment. "You know what? I think I will ask Him to tell me a joke."

"Seriously?"

"Yes. I will ask Him the next time we talk."

At that point, I was feeling quite pleased with myself. And secretly, I couldn't wait to hear that joke. Of course, I wasn't expecting God to *actually* tell Ravi a joke, but even the thought of asking God for one struck me as hilarious.

A few days went by, and during the filming a lot of crazy stuff went down. But toward the end of our time together I asked Ravi about the joke. He told me he kept forgetting, that every time God talked to him it had been all business. Shoot, it was enough for Ravi simply to remember everything God was telling him.

So I headed back home to Chicago. But every few days I sent an email to Ravi to see if he had asked God for a joke. He kept telling me no, he had not had the chance to bring it up. I got busy with life again, and a few weeks went by. One day I remembered that I hadn't asked Ravi in a while, so I wrote him again. This time he told me that, actually, yes, he did ask God for a joke.

And?

He told Ravi one.

And?

Ravi wasn't going to tell me the joke.

I could have punched my computer screen. I begged, I pleaded, but to no avail. Ravi refused to tell me.

I asked him if it was at least funny.

He said yes, kind of.

At that point, my curiosity was raised to the boiling point. I was never going to let this die. So when our good mutual friend Will Hart (whom I filmed with in *Furious Love*) told me a few months later that he was heading over to India to see Ravi, I told him the story and instructed him to get Ravi to tell him the joke. He promised to get it out of him (he has known Ravi much longer).

When Will returned, I called him immediately.

"Wilson," he said, "he's not going to tell you that joke."

"Why not?"

"I don't know, but he wouldn't even tell me. I have no idea what his problem is."

More months went by, and Ravi came to visit me in Chicago. Now I had him cornered. I was like a rabid dog, hell-bent on prying that stupid joke out of my friend. It was no longer simple curiosity driving me, but raving madness.

"Ravi, you have to tell me the joke."

"I cannot tell you the joke, sir."

"But it's my joke! You wouldn't have even asked for it if I hadn't told you to. If anyone on earth deserves to hear this joke, it's me!"

"I can't."

"Why?"

And that's when I started to get an inkling as to why he wouldn't tell me.

"Well," Ravi began, a little warily, "I asked Him, and He kind of laughed."

"He laughed?"

"Well, it was kind of a giggle."

"God giggles?"

"Yeah, like a cross between a laugh and a giggle. I could tell He thought the idea was funny. So He was quiet for a moment, then He starts telling me a joke. It starts off really funny, and I'm laughing. It was a story joke, you know? But as He's telling the story, it keeps getting more and more funny, and I'm laughing out loud. But then it gets to the punch line and . . ."

"Yeah?"

"And I realized it was a joke about me."

I stared at him for a moment. Have to admit, I wasn't expecting that. So God told Ravi a joke, but it was a joke about Ravi. And then I understood why he was never going to tell me. Ravi is an intensely private person. He knew that if he ever told me the joke I'd probably wind up putting it in one of my books (which I would—and, in fact, did), and the last thing this humble, private man wanted was for the whole world to read the one recorded joke told by God in human history, and he's the punch line.

This also shows the genius of God. He granted my request, but in such a way as to make sure the joke He told never saw the light of day. It was a personal moment between two friends, and it was intended to stay that way. While I'm disappointed, a big part of me is more than a little satisfied to know that the God I love and serve actually told a joke.

And that I made Him giggle.

So what's the point of all this? When we look at God's character as displayed through His creation of the world and His first interactions with the men and women He created, we can understand that, from the very beginning, He has been a God who desires friendship with us. He is not an absentee landlord. Nor is He some deity up in the sky, looking down at this world with clinical distance. He is a God who desires to walk with us in the cool of the day; whose first act toward us was a kiss; who sees us as more than just worker bees; and who is far more relatable than we give Him credit for.

In essence, He is a God who, if nothing else, shows us right from the start that He actually *has* a character; He *has* a personality. It is up to us, then, to discover it.

3

Trust Never Looked So Frightening

As I was growing up in church, there were a few stories in the Bible that scared me to death. This really hindered any chance of my walking too closely with God. It had nothing to do with the actual stories (as we will soon see) but rather came from the interpretation of those stories—in large part because the one doing the interpreting was a sixteen-year-old kid with no real experience of the Father's heart.

The granddaddy of them all, and the story that honestly kept me at a safe distance from the Father for the longest time, was Abraham's near sacrifice of Isaac. As I speak in more and more churches, I find that I am not alone in my reaction to this story. In fact, it has become something of an epidemic among Christians. Let's look at the story as a whole first.

A Freaky Premise

Here is Abraham, minding his own business when God shows up and tells him He's going to make a great nation out of him: "I will make your descendants as the dust of the earth; so that if a man could number the dust of the earth, then your descendants also could be numbered" (Genesis 13:16).

Be there any doubt that God likes to show that He is God, consider this as Exhibit A. He doesn't find a handsome, virile man of 26 to tell this to. No, that would be far too easy for God. Instead, he finds an old man of 75 who already has everything in the world (he was very wealthy) *except* for the one thing he couldn't control. He has no children. And then, just to add a little fuel to the fire, God *waits 25 more years* before He tells Abraham that it's now time to start having kids.

You know the story. Abraham and Sarah indeed do have a son, Isaac, when they're crazy old, and he is the joy of Abraham's life. But then one day God comes to Abraham and asks him to sacrifice Isaac on an altar, and Abraham agrees to do it. They go on a three-day journey, Isaac carries the wood, and just before Abraham plunges the knife into his son's heart, God stops him and tells him it was all just a test. Here, sacrifice this ram instead. Everyone goes home happy, and we Christians learn a great lesson on what faith is supposed to look like.

But here's the problem with this story. It , , , well . . it comes across as a little twisted. We like to water down what is really going on here because the reality of the situation is horrific. We use the word *sacrifice* because that sounds a lot better than *murder*. And the message from God? "Oh, you love your kid more than anything in the world? Tell you what. Walk him out to the woods and cut out his heart. That will prove to Me that you love Me." When you get down to brass tacks, this story seems wrong on many levels.

It was this story more than any other that made me terrified of God for most of my life.

I'm Not Giving *That* Up

The Christian faith is, at its core, about just that. Faith. We worship Someone who is invisible. We believe that Jesus did what the Bible says He did, that God loves us, that we're going to heaven when we die, and a whole bunch of other things. We are told to have faith when we pray, faith when we are persecuted, faith when we are lonely, sad or abused. Faith, faith, faith. It's the cornerstone of all that we hold dear. And in the Bible, Abraham is held up as the shining example of what that faith looks like.

Maybe Abraham was cut from very different cloth. Maybe he was a hard man, singularly focused, lacking emotion. I have no doubt it was difficult for him to agree to kill his own son, but the fact that he even entertained the idea seems so outlandish to me that I have a hard time relating to him in any meaningful way. If God came to me and asked me to kill

43

one of my kids, I'd probably stop believing in Him. What kind of a God would ask us to do such a thing?

This is the way my mind used to work regarding this story, and it was the reason I didn't trust God for most of my life. How can you possibly trust a God like this? The story of Abraham and Isaac simply showed that if you choose to get radical with God, He is going to ask radical things of you;. and you are probably going to have to give up the thing you love the most.

After all, giving up what you love—"laying it down at the altar"—is supposed to be the highest calling of a Christian. And those who sacrifice the most become the shining examples to the rest of us—they're the ones who come back home from the mission field and speak in our churches and tell us stories about what God is doing through them since they sold everything and headed to Zimbabwe or wherever, and we sit in our seats feeling like total spiritual losers because we just cannot envision life without cable TV. So we give our money to these people, hoping that will ease our guilt a bit, but we go through life knowing that we're called to so much more, but scared to death of what that "more" might look like.

And why are we scared? Because of stories like Abraham and Isaac! I don't want to give up my kids. I don't want to give up my dreams. My promises. My passions. But if I give Him everything (as they tell me I'm supposed to), that's exactly what I'm going to have to do. Because that's what God does. He asks for everything.

So for the longest time, I viewed this story as a story of Abraham, and it was supposed to show me his character and how amazing the guy was. And to some extent that is true. But the more I discover about God, the more I'm beginning to realize that this story is more about God's heart and His character than anything. And far from implying that He is a sadistic practical joker, it actually reveals a very tender, very loving personality.

The Friendship Connection

Over the years I've spent making films, God has taught me many lessons, but none has been impressed upon me more than the fact that He desires relationship with us beyond anything else. Unfortunately, though, much of His Church falls short of His desire. Sometimes we try to placate our guilt for being terrible Christians by overworking ourselves and volunteering for everything; sometimes we pleasantly keep God at arm's length, thinking all is well.

Basically we are acquaintances with God. We go to His house once a week. We eat with Him occasionally. Once in a while we actually talk to Him, and we know other people who are really good friends with Him. We've had just enough interaction with Him over the years that we can confidently say that we know Him and that He knows us.

But as we all know, there is a big difference between an acquaintance and a friend. While an acquaintance sees you once in a while and knows a few things about you, a true friend knows you intimately. You will trust that friend with your life. When God talks about wanting to spew lukewarm believers out of His mouth, it doesn't take a rocket scientist to figure out what He means by lukewarm. Not hot, like a close friend. Not cold, like a stranger. But lukewarm, like an acquaintance. Crap.

I've said many times before that most of my life was spent holding God at bay—keeping my distance from Him, but remaining close enough to say I knew Him well enough to (1) get into heaven and (2) be able to say there were other Christians out there who were far worse. And that was really the point of the whole game back then. As long as I did enough stuff I could remain in the club as a member of good standing. It was like a checklist of sorts: quiet time, Bible reading, church attendance, small group, no cussing. Keep a regular habit of those things, and you get your "Good Christian" card punched each year. The problem is, all of those things are simply things you do. They don't in and of themselves lead you to intimacy.

Don't misunderstand me. Disciplines are important to growth and maturity in Christ. But when they become duty as opposed to something done out of relationship, that's when you're beginning to practice "religion" in the bad sense. When you begin to think that you're in right standing with God because of what you *do*, as opposed to what He *did*, that's when you know you're in trouble. But, of course, you don't know you're in trouble because you *think* you're doing great! It's a slippery slope that is as dangerous as it is innocuous.

But what does all this have to do with Abraham almost murdering his son? Well, I think the reason we often turn to doing things *for* God as opposed to doing them *with* Him is because we want to keep Him at a safe distance but still walk forward with the Christian life. Knowing about Him is a lot different from truly knowing Him, and a friend who doesn't trust is far different from a friend who trusts with everything.

And trust, ultimately, is what this whole story of Abraham is about. Trust is what the whole Bible is about! If God is after relationship, and the most important aspect of a relationship is trust, then God must desire our trust in Him more than anything else. My wife and I can have all the passion in the world for each other, but if there is an inherent lack of trust between us, our relationship will always be stunted. You can love your parents, but if you don't trust them it drives a wedge between you that keeps your relationship from truly thriving. Trust means everything to God, because it is the last hurdle we must jump before we can step into true intimacy with Him.

I always loved God, but I never trusted Him. How can you trust someone who at any moment could ask you to give up the thing you love the most, just to prove your love for Him? That is not a trustworthy God, no matter how you want to sugarcoat it. But that understanding of God was rooted in my own spiritual immaturity. My view of God was one-sided. I thought He wanted me to serve Him, when in reality He wanted me to befriend Him.

In any friendship, there are escalating levels of connection as you go through life together. That's why your friendships with those you've known for twenty years are so much stronger than those you've known for three weeks. The connection between two people grows over time and through mutual understanding and experiences. And the same is true in our friendship with God. My problem was that I viewed a fifty-year friendship (God and Abraham) through a three-week friendship (me and God) lens.

God Dips His Toe in the Friendship Water

In Genesis 12, God gives the first call to Abraham. They are not friends yet, but for whatever reason God has His eyes on this guy. So He comes to Abraham (at that point he was still Abram), and, in essence, tests the waters of Abraham's heart with His first-ever request. He tells Abraham to leave the land he is in and go to "the land I will show you." This is the most basic of instructions, and while it certainly calls for some level of trust and commitment, it's not entirely earth-shattering in its demands. I'm sure Abraham asked the question "Where are we going?" to which God could simply answer, "Just trust Me."

Unfortunately, most people don't even get beyond this call from God! Change your course, change your city, change your job, etc., is met typically with skepticism, fear and outright rejection. "That couldn't be God," we say, "I must have heard Him wrong." Or, the prospect of the unknown is simply too frightening so we do our "spiritual stalling" by lining up numerous things that have to happen first before we will be sufficiently satisfied that we have received enough "confirmation" from God to move forward.

Genesis 12:4 gives Abraham's response. "So Abram departed as the LORD had spoken to him."

Abraham's response was immediate obedience. When God calls us to obedience and a life of trust, He will almost never toss us into the deep end. Not because we can't handle it, but rather because He must be certain that we can be trusted with the enormity of our true destiny. God's dreams for us are always going to be so much bigger and more spectacular than we could ever dream of, because God is incapable of dreaming small. I mean, He's God. Even His small dreams would be outrageously huge to us! So He has dreams for each of us, but His dreams can only become a reality if we become willing parties to them. Unfortunately for most of us, becoming a willing party requires trusting in a God we often find untrustworthy.

As an example of this checking-out period when God looks to see if we're up for the challenge of the dreams He has for us, just look at Jesus' Parable of the Ten Minas in Luke 19. The master gives ten servants the same amount to start with, and it is pretty evident he is doing so to see which of these men can be trusted with the most. These guys all get the same gift and then go off and do whatever it is they do with that gift, based on their ability as well as their tenacity and commitment.

The master then returns and asks to see what they've been able to do with what he gave them. The servant who is most fruitful and trustworthy gets the extra talent from the servant who proves to be a bum. To the one who gained the most, the master gives *more*. It's the natural order of how God operates. You want the great things I have for you? Then let's go through the steps to get there. Most of us either wimp out when the steps seem beyond us, or we stop when we are satisfied with what we have already been given.

One interesting point about the trustworthy servant getting more: God is not just generous; He's also a great businessman.

A Budding Friendship

Genesis 13 gives us a further glimpse into Abraham's growing trust in the Lord, and you can sense their relationship blossoming. Once again, God tells Abraham to look around because He is giving him the land as far as he can see in all directions. Then,

> Abram moved his tent, and went and dwelt by the terebinth trees of Mamre, which are in Hebron, and built an altar there to the LORD.

verse 18

It will be many years before we listen in on another conversation between God and Abraham, but this nugget shows the beginning of a beautiful friendship. God promises Abraham a wonderful gift, and Abraham builds an altar where he can commune with God daily. What happens between them over the next few years is lost to history—but you can believe that Abraham continues to grow in faith and favor.

Their relationship takes a great leap forward, possibly years later, when Abraham is asking who will be his heir to receive all these promises God is making.

> The word of the LORD came to him, saying, "This one [Abram's servant] shall not be your heir, but one who will come from your own body shall be your heir." Then He brought him outside and said, "Look now toward heaven, and count the stars if you are able to number them." And He said to him, "So shall your descendants be." And he believed in the LORD, and He accounted it to him for righteousness.

Genesis 15:4–6

Because Abraham believes God, their friendship enters a new level. It is now deep enough for God to trust this man (he is, after all, believing the impossible) with His next big move, one that will affect all of human history. That very night, God makes a covenant with Abraham where He seals the deal in a way that is both legally and cosmically binding. They have now moved past the stage of simply talking to each other and dreaming together. Once Abraham believes God for the impossible simply because God says He will do it, things start to get real.

After this event, a full 25 years pass before God's promise finally comes to fruition. Abraham's character and his friendship with God have to grow to the point where he will be ready to step into the destiny God is calling him to. Yet both Abraham and Sarah show they are fully human with human emotions when both of them react to God's promise of a child with laughter. It is innocent enough, but God does make a point to call them on it when He asks Sarah why she laughed (see Genesis 18:13). God may giggle, but when He makes a promise He is deadly serious.

The next few verses in the story show how far the relationship between God and Abraham has progressed. If you recall, God comes to Abraham at his tent, accompanied by two other angels, and announces that by this time next year, Sarah will have given birth to a baby boy. He then turns His attention to the other reason He has come on this day: Sodom and Gomorrah. When God has finished informing Abraham and Sarah about their coming son, He makes an extraordinary remark: "Then the men rose from there and looked toward Sodom, and Abraham went with them to send them on the way. And the LORD said, 'Shall I hide from Abraham what I am doing?'" (Genesis 18:16–17).

This leads into the famous conversation in which Abraham bargains with God, banking on the fact that God will not "sweep away the righteous with the wicked" in the city. Asking first if God will spare the city if only fifty righteous people can be found, Abraham whittles down the number to just ten. God agrees not to destroy Sodom and Gomorrah if He can find just ten people there who are righteous.

The fact that God listens to Abraham's pleas for mercy and recalculates His plans according to Abraham's wishes is amazing enough! You would think that God has His mind made up here, yet His friend steps in and, since he is a very close friend, God chooses to listen to him. But that whole episode wouldn't even exist if God had not considered Abraham such a good friend in the first place. "Shall I hide from Abraham what I am doing?" This is God admitting that He is standing next to a man whom He trusts so much and cares for so much, that it just wouldn't be right to keep His plans from him.

This is friendship at its deepest level. Abraham is perhaps the only person in the world at this point that God is willing to reveal His plans to, which is precisely the reason He listens to Abraham when he begs for mercy upon the unsuspecting city.

Interestingly, as soon as this conversation is over and chapter 19 begins, there are no longer three individuals heading for the cities, but now only two. God comes in the form of a man to speak with His friend, but He does not go down into the cities to see the wickedness firsthand. He expresses to Abraham knowledge of their grievous sin (see Genesis 18:20), and I can think of nothing worse than wicked men trying to anally rape the God of the universe (see Genesis 19:5). I wonder if God ultimately sends the angels, choosing not to go Himself, because His holiness would rage so violently against the wickedness that it would have incinerated Lot and his house as well as everyone else in the city. Of course, it also speaks to what He cares about most: His friends are far more important to Him than the judgment of sinners!

Death to What You Love

But now we must get to the crux of this story, the part that caused my trust in God to be eroded. I couldn't believe He could ask such a thing. But again, this was before I really got to know Him and began to understand His character as portrayed in the Scriptures.

Genesis 21:34 states that "Abraham stayed in the land of the Philistines many days." Isaac has just been born and weaned, so we can assume that a number of years go by before that fateful moment. This gives Abraham even more time to grow in his appreciation and love for God. And the core of his life (Isaac) is a daily reminder of God's goodness and faithfulness to him. So the day Abraham receives the call to kill Isaac, the boy is no longer a boy, but is instead at least a teenager or possibly even a young man in his early twenties.

I often wonder about Isaac when I ponder this story. Abraham gets all the glory, but Isaac may face the worst of the testing. Obviously he doesn't know what his father is up to, since he asks where the lamb is that they will be sacrificing, to which his father replies in faith, "The Lord will provide." But once they arrive at the rock and Abraham reveals his plan, the storyteller in me can't help but wonder how that scene played out.

Was there a struggle? Was there a shouting match? Did Abraham have to sit with his son and remind him of all the promises of God, and all that God had done for them, and that this, too, would turn out okay? We know that Abraham knew that child sacrifice was an abomination to God (see Deuteronomy 12:30–31), and he also believed that God could raise Isaac from the dead (see Hebrews 11:19). Were both men banking on that as Isaac lay down on the rock and his father tied him up? We'll probably never know for sure, but we do know that whatever happened, Isaac voluntarily offered himself up as a sacrifice to God.

And then there is Sarah. Where is she in this story? I am assuming Abraham never told his wife what he was about to do—an assumption based on the fact that he didn't tell his son. Maybe she stayed home because she thought this was just the boys going out on a three-day father/son camping trip. Maybe she knew she wouldn't be able to bear watching this.

Again, we'll never know, but it is clear that Abraham's faith is not the only one being tested here. He is the primary focus of the story because this is the final piece in an ultimate act of a trusting friendship, but it seems that Abraham had also built a level of trust in God throughout his family. His is not a solitary faith meant only for him. It has to spill out onto those around him.

The day finally comes. After so many years of growing together, trusting each other, loving each other and bonding together, God comes to Abraham and asks him, quite matter-of-factly, to take his son to Mount Moriah and murder him there as an offering.

This has to be one of the biggest bombshells in the entire Bible. The son Abraham wanted more than anything, the very one through whom all the promises of God are to come, the person he loves the most—God is asking Abraham to kill him. Let me lay my cards on the table right now and admit that I have three children, and I could never do this. Not in any way, shape or form could I ever take one of my children on a three-day journey where, upon arriving at the destination, I would then take a knife and stab that child through the heart. It feels like a scene from a highly disturbing, dark movie. I wouldn't even consider it. But Abraham, this complete stud and by now a seasoned friend of God, knowing that God would never ask something of him without reason, purpose or the motivation of love behind it, agrees.

Even more amazingly, Abraham "rose early in the morning" (Genesis 22:3). He doesn't stew in his juices, hem and haw, or come up with lots of excuses as to why he must put this off for a little bit. Instead, he plunges into God's request almost immediately. He is almost robotic in his response, but that, I think, is a misleading representation. If your closest Friend of fifty years comes to you and asks you for something that means the world to him, you will drop everything and do whatever he asks. Abraham is simply responding to his Friend, as a friend.

He saddles his donkey, takes his son and two servants and heads toward the mountain God has called him to. How many of the things God calls us to feel like actual mountains that must be overcome? There is some level of work involved in any loving relationship, so we can never assume that life with God will simply be one uninterrupted honeymoon. There will be a passion from Him that never fades, for sure, but there will also be times when He calls us even deeper into His heart, and we must work to move forward because standing still, remaining the same, is always what our flesh wants.

When they reach the mountain, Abraham reveals his intent. He turns to his servants and says, "Stay here. We're going up there to sacrifice to God, and in a little while, we'll come back." This tells us all we need to know about Abraham. His faith is unshakeable, even after three full days with only his thoughts, wondering if he heard right, wondering if he's totally gone off the deep end. Where most of us would crumble as we approach the hardest decision of our lives, Abraham embraces it, because he knows his God is good and would call him only to good things. He fully believes he will be walking back to these men with his son at his side. How that will happen, who knows? But Scripture tells us that he believed Isaac would be resurrected. Whatever happens, Abraham believes in God over his own understanding, and *that* is the key to friendship with God.

We know the rest of the story. Throughout the episode, Abraham moves forward with steely determination. He never wavers from his mission. He ties his son up. He takes out a knife. He raises it in the air. You wonder if at this point his son screams. You wonder if there are tears in Abraham's eyes, if his son has changed his mind and is pleading with his father to spare his life. You wonder what is going on in Abraham's mind, if he can't believe what he is about to do. But his mind is obviously made up, because God knows his thoughts, knows his determination, knows that he is actually about to kill his own son. And that's when God steps in and stops it all. He has seen enough. And He is thoroughly impressed.

Friendship Is Serious Business

As much as I wanted to impress God, I was always afraid of Him as a result of this story because this God seemed to be playing a cruel game. As much as I was impressed with Abraham, I was more horrified at God. He was a God who asked for the things we loved the most. How could I trust Him if I knew that whatever I loved, He'd be asking me, at some point, to kill it?

But again, I did not understand His nature, His character or His heart. I viewed this story as an outsider of sorts—as one views another family's squabble, seeing just the absurdity of the actions and not understanding the nuances of the relationships. God was about to change all of human history through one man, and, on one level, He needed to show the world what this man was made of so they would know what kind of stuff they came from. But to me, that is far secondary to the real nature of what is going on here.

This is a story about friendship, trust and, ultimately, love. God's love is not something to be taken lightly because He has invested everything, literally, into loving us. Our understanding of God's love is clouded by our own inability to love people well or consistently. Sometimes we have bad days. Sometimes we have bad years! Our love is fickle, often based on our temperaments or personalities, and is typically not at all unconditional. Since we're so bad at loving others, it becomes nearly impossible for us to understand God's love for us, which is not fickle, conditional or swaying in any way.

We simply do not take love as seriously as God does. But serious He is—deadly serious, in fact, and His burning desire for intimacy with us keeps Him always on the lookout, His eyes running to and fro across the earth, for someone who is willing to go to the next level in his or her relationship with Him (see 2 Chronicles 16:9). When someone makes that commitment, the journey of trust and friendship begins officially. To the outside observer, these "radicals" grow increasingly bold in their trust of God, and that terrifies the rest of us who have a hard time trusting Him at all. All we see is the hardship and sacrifice being offered up by God's good friends, and we say it's too scary, too much to ask.

For those who are growing in friendship with God, this is not frightening at all. Instead, it becomes the most natural response in the world. As He proves Himself over and over again, we grow more and more dependent on Him, more and more trusting of Him, and after a few years we look back and can't imagine doing life any other way.

But, still, what about God in this story? What do we do with a God who, even if He never intended for Abraham to kill his son, would even *ask* such a thing from him? We understand that this was all a big, elaborate test for Abraham, but isn't this test crossing the line? I used to think so.

Imagine that I bought my wife a puppy. Imagine, then, that puppy becoming the central focus of her life. Every day she doted on it, worried about it, talked about it, went shopping for it and basically obsessed about its well-being from sunrise to sunset, spending more time with the puppy than with me.

As her husband, it would be entirely within my rights to ask her if she would be willing to get rid of the puppy in favor of me. If she said no, I would know that she officially loved the puppy more than she loved me. If she said yes, I would equally know where I stood in the pecking order. Even though this was a gift from me, I would never want one of my gifts to outshine my relationship with her.

Isaac was a gift from God to Abraham. He was never supposed to happen; it was a pure miracle that he was even born. But when God asks Abraham to sacrifice his son, He throws in the line "your only son Isaac, whom you love." God knows that there is only one thing now competing with Abraham's affection for Him in the world, and if they are going to have the deepest relationship possible, there can be *nothing* that competes. God is not just testing Abraham's faith; He is testing his love.

Before you cry foul and say, "But it is still too much to ask," remember whom you're dealing with here. God is all in. We're the ones whose love is fickle and weak. God's love is not. We think it's such a horrible thing that He would ask a man to murder his son just to show how much he loves God, yet that is *precisely* what God did for us! God murdered His own Son: "It was the LORD's will to crush him" (Isaiah 53:10 NIV) so He could finally have us all to Himself. The only thing standing between us and Him, from His side of things, was our sin. So He decided to offer salvation once and for all by not only killing His Son, but doing so in the most brutal, horrific way possible.

Don't ever doubt God's commitment to you. He has already proven it. What He asks of you will never compare to what He has already asked of Himself.

God's Invisibility Cloak

Ever since I was a little boy, I've wondered what God looks like. At first I figured He was just like a puff of smoke, since He was a "spirit" and didn't have flesh and blood like me, but then I remembered reading in Genesis that He decided to make man in His "image," whatever that meant. I would have internal debates about whether He was talking about the essence of Himself or, you know, His hair color. Was this "image" something internal, something that could not be quantified, per se, but that everyone will be able to recognize when we get to heaven and see Him outright? Or does God have hairy armpits like me?

Maybe it's just my odd mind at work, but if, by some chance, we aren't the only ones He created, and out there in the vastness of the universe is another life form, another planet and another people He is trying to have relationship with, would He have created them in His image as well, or would He have thought about throwing a curve ball, spicing things up a bit? These are the things I ponder, and they are probably the stupidest things I could spend my time pondering.

But even as a child I wondered what God looked like, and I'm pretty sure I'm not the only one. Quite often for me it has simply been a case of pure, unadulterated curiosity. Is He absolutely enormous? For a long time, whenever I thought about heaven I pictured billions of people worshiping at the throne, and two big feet sitting there. Like He's so big we can't even see the top of Him. And of course He wears sandals in this vision, because everything we acquaint with the Almighty always has to adhere to the clothing and customs of the Middle East.

But then, God existed long before Israel did, so I wonder if He had some kind of different, unique, funky style until He became such good friends with Abraham and Moses. And then did they affect Him so much that they actually changed His choice of fashion? What are we going to do if we get to heaven and the Father is rocking some Adidas? Maybe He changes it up all the time: a little Nike here, some flip-flops there, an occasional Dutch wooden clog. I told you my mind goes to weird places sometimes.

While I certainly do jest (sort of), there is a very real concept here that I think deserves some attention. God *does* look like something. He *does* have a form and a body (of some sort). We can conjecture all we want, and paint pictures of old men with beards sitting on clouds, but the fact remains that God is real and, as such, has a form and shape. And I can't believe that I'm the only one who has wondered why in the world He doesn't just show Himself.

One of the great frustrations for me as a Christian (as well as a filmmaker) is the fact that I have to try to convince people to fall in love and believe in someone who is invisible. When I was having my own personal spiritual crisis in my twenties, wondering if God was even real and, if so, why this Christianity He created was so boring and lame (*Just go to church, be a good person and believe the right things? Really? That's it?*), I would often ask Him to show Himself. Give me five seconds. That's all I need for a lifetime of devoted service. Just a quick glimpse, even if it's just one of those sandaled feet of Yours. But of course I'd stare at nothing and sink deeper into my existential despair.

But then I started making movies about God, and I started seeing Him move on people right before my eyes. I would see impossible things happen to people as if an invisible person walked up to them and did something to them. As I saw more and more evidence of Him, I thought about seeing Him physically less and less. As I became better friends with Him, I started to understand His personality more, His character; the need to see with my physical eyes waned. It hasn't totally left, but it isn't front and center the way it used to be.

But until recently, I never stopped wondering why it has to be this way. Why does God choose to remain invisible? The whole world would believe if, just for a few seconds, He revealed Himself to everyone. Imagine how much suffering, how many bad choices and prodigal stories could be avoided with a simple pulling back of the divine invisibility cloak. Why not just do it then?

The answer, I think, lies in the one time in all of history that He actually *did* do this. . . .

Crazy Favor

Aside from the Garden of Eden, when God walked in the flesh with Adam and Eve in the cool of the day and (probably) told them jokes, there is one instance in the Bible when God revealed His true form. Something like this is reserved for only the closest and dearest of friends, and while David gets the prize for being the man after God's own heart, Moses gets to be God's best friend.

Exodus 33:18–23 is a thrilling narrative where one man finds himself in the peculiar position of, in a sense, finding God in a really good mood toward him, and, in return, he goes for broke and asks for the moon.

If you recall, the Israelites have just committed the golden calf sin, and Moses has interceded with God to spare them. Yes, they're morons, he tells God, but they're Your morons. God relents on account of Moses, and then makes this re-markable statement: "I will also do this thing that you have spoken; for you have found grace in My sight, and I know you by name" (verse 17).

Let's go into this scene, shall we?

God is angry going into this conversation. He is ready to slaughter this "stiff-necked people" and start all over again with Moses as the new Abraham. Moses, in a sense, calms God down. (Before you get angry and write me a nasty email admonishing me for writing that, remember: This is Old

Covenant here, and Jesus' death has permanently calmed God down.) And now they're having a good old-fashioned lovefest together. God tells Moses, essentially, that he's His favorite, and that they're good friends ("I know you by name").

This is an example where reading stories in the Bible without imagination can ruin the richness of the event. Typically we read that and move on to the next verse—which, in my opinion, feels a little out of place: "And [Moses] said, 'Please, show me Your glory'" (verse 18).

So we typically read that, and continue to move on in the story. But enter the scene, and really think about what is happening here, and it blows your mind (at least it blows mine). God is mad. He's just gone out on a limb and chosen this crew as His special kids. He does incredible stuff for them, and makes all kinds of promises to them—not for anything they've done, but just because He loves them—and they return the favor by worshiping a statue. It would be like me going above and beyond to bless my kids, even when they've been pretty rotten and don't deserve it, and they take my blessing, walk outside and thank a tree.

But Moses pleads with God to have mercy when mercy has not been earned, and God, because He is slow to anger and rich in mercy, affirms Moses' plea. He listens to him because Moses is a friend.

I can see this scene playing out, and I put myself in Moses' shoes at that moment. It has to be a momentous situation. The God of the universe has just listened to you and has just opened His heart to you. There's a lot of goodwill happening here, and Moses must have realized that he is never going to have a chance as good as this again. He's heard the voice, but he's never seen the speaker. So he goes for broke and blurts out the biblical equivalent of "Can I please see what You look like?"

It's the question that every human in history who has believed in God has thought at some point or another. What does God look like? And here Moses just goes for it. And what does God do? He says yes! Of course, He tells Moses that He will not show His face, because if He did that Moses would certainly die (apparently pure goodness would make your head explode). But this is interesting, too, for the mere fact that it proves beyond a doubt that God actually *has* a face! He actually looks like something.

He says:

> "I will make all My goodness pass before you, and I will proclaim the name of the LORD before you. . . . Here is a place by Me, and you shall stand on the rock. So it shall be, while My glory passes by, that I will put you in the cleft of the rock, and will cover you with My hand while I pass by. Then I will take away My hand, and you shall see My back."
>
> Exodus 33:19, 21–23

This reveals two interesting points about God:

1. God apparently can exist in a particular spot. I believe He is everywhere and in everything, but, at the same time, in some way, He can *be* somewhere in particular.
2. Not only does God give Moses what he asks for, but He gives him *more* than he asks for! Moses never asks God to speak His name, but God does it anyway. Most likely it is because God's glory does not reside just in His person, but also in His voice (we have noted that everything is subject to it, because through His voice

66

the whole universe was created), as well as His name, which defines and represents Him. And, of course, the true heart of God is always to give to us abundantly beyond what we even ask for.

We know the rest of the story. God passes by, gives Moses a little speech about how amazingly patient yet devoted to righteousness He is, then shows Moses His back. They chat some more, God gives Moses more of the Law, and then Moses heads down the mountain back to the people.

The Reason Why

When Moses arrives back home, everyone freaks out because his face is shining. They make him put a veil over his face because. . . . Actually, I don't know why. Was it scary? Was it too disconcerting? Did it hurt their eyes? The Bible is never clear on the Israelites' problem with Moses' glowing face, but that's not really the point here. The point is the very reason why God *must* remain invisible.

If just seeing God's back causes a man's face to glow and an entire people group to become so uncomfortable that they make him cover it up, imagine what would happen if God showed Himself in any real, physical way. God is so powerful and so irresistible that if He did show Himself, we would be powerless not to bow to Him and worship Him.

But God is not looking for people who are so impressed with His physicality that they bow to Him reflexively. He is looking for relationship in the deepest sense of the word. While it makes things infinitely harder for Him to woo us and draw us to His heart, invisibility is the only way to make sure that our love for Him is genuine and wholly our choice. Once He reveals Himself, the whole world will bow before Him, and the gig is up (see Isaiah 45:23). But until that day, He's going to dedicate His entire existence to trying to get you to fall in love with someone you can't see.

So why must God remain invisible? The answer is simple. Love. It is another side of His character that should impress even the most jaded heart. While showing Himself would speed everything up and make a relationship inevitable, God chooses to do it the hard way so that you and I have the right of refusal. He's not going to force Himself on anyone, because that goes against everything that love is.

The one guy in history who got to peek behind the curtain did so only because he had a relationship with the Almighty in a way no one else ever has. God does not honor our service to Him as much as He honors our relationship with Him.

Too often, though, we think it's the other way around.

5

God's Best Friend

Pound for pound, Moses seems to me to be the biggest stud in the Bible (next to Jesus, of course). The guy had the whole package: outrageous testimony, crazy miracle encounters and he can actually hold the title of God's best friend. It's easy to see why so many movies have been made about him.

But this book isn't about unpacking the lives of various characters in the Bible as much as it is about understanding more of God's own character through His interaction with these characters of His. As I've already mentioned, God is not a distant, logic-obsessed deity who is cold and calculating. He is, instead, a loving Father who must fight through the nearly impossible barrier of invisibility and our hostile hearts in an attempt to enter into a loving, caring and intimate relationship with us. Moses may have exemplified the extreme of this relationship, which is why we have so much to learn from his friendship with God.

So many of God's greatest characters in His story are murderers, con artists, swindlers and scoundrels, and we tend to gloss over this fact when we read the Bible or teach Sunday school. The reality, when you think about it, is somewhat disturbing.

Take Moses, for instance. We all know his birth story. He is saved from infanticide by his quick-thinking mother and sister, is adopted into Pharaoh's family and grows up privileged and wealthy. God skips over Moses' adolescence right up to the point where things start to get juicy. The fact that God includes an act of cold-blooded murder in Moses' story should tip us off to something in and of itself.

> One day, when Moses had grown up, he went out to his people and looked on their burdens, and he saw an Egyptian beating a Hebrew, one of his people. He looked this way and that, and seeing no one, he struck down the Egyptian and hid him in the sand.
>
> Exodus 2:11–12 ESV

The first time we see Moses after he is rescued by the princess, he is taking a leisurely walk to see "his people." We can assume he realizes he is different from his Egyptian family, and adheres to some kind of personal pride that he is an Israelite. I wonder if his mother instilled this in him as a young boy, when she was chosen by the princess to nurse him. Who knows, really. All we know for sure is that Moses lived among the elite of Egyptian society, yet never fully let go of his Israelite heritage.

While on this stroll, he sees an Egyptian beating an Israel-ite, and this is where things get interesting. He kills the Egyptian and buries his body in the sand. Does anyone else find this act of his a little excessive? Once again, let's jump into literary conjecture here based on story/character psychology.

Moses was the adopted grandson of Pharaoh, so one can assume that he had a bit of clout in the kingdom. It is perfectly legitimate to think that he simply needed to approach this Egyptian taskmaster and order him to stand down. Or, if he wished to ensure the safety of his kinsman, he could have gone over the man's head and had him removed from his position of authority.

He could have done any number of things to help out his fellow Israelite, but instead he chose (possibly) to pick up a rock and bash the man's skull in like some kind of Martin Scorsese movie. This was cold-blooded murder, plain and simple. He was not defending himself. This was not justi-fied. And it was illegal and punishable by death. Why, then, did Moses do it?

To do something this extreme, a person probably has some fairly high levels of rage and pent-up anger. We know noth-ing of Moses up to this point. All we know is that he sees a guy beating another guy, snaps, and goes hells bells on his cranium. As I try to put myself in his shoes, I wonder if this is simply the boiling-over point of something that has been simmering inside of Moses for years.

He is different from his family, and I'm sure he is reminded of it every day. He looks different; he is a stepchild who is probably not fully embraced like the other children around him; and his people are all slaves. Maybe he is angry that

71

he was kept from his mother. Maybe he is simply so righteous minded that resentment toward the Egyptians in regard to his people has been building since his teens. Maybe he's frustrated with the idea that he feels he has no purpose in life. Whatever it is, it seems likely that this is not an out-of-the-blue moment of aggression with no history behind it. Murder almost never is.

Why am I bringing all of this up? What does this have to do with God's character? Well, everything! Because, you see, this conflicted, angry, frustrated young man was the very man, of all the people on the planet, that God chose to be His nearest and dearest friend.

The Good Kid

When I was growing up, I was always a really good kid. I never got into trouble, never did much of anything wrong and always listened to my parents. I didn't go to parties, didn't do drugs or drink and didn't mess around with girls. I was the guy at church that every mother wanted her daughter to date, but one whom none of the girls wanted to go out with. I wasn't dangerous enough, good-looking enough or interesting enough. I guess the acne could have played a small part as well.

Because I never got into trouble, I figured God was fairly happy with me. I didn't avoid bad things because my heart wanted to please Him, but rather because I was scared to death of the consequences—both from my parents and from God. I knew if I ever went too far with a girl, she was going to get pregnant. I knew if I ever did drugs, I'd most likely OD. I knew if I ever tried to steal something, I'd definitely wind up in jail. So it wasn't righteousness that kept me out of trouble, but fear (which, I'll admit, in these circumstances, probably wasn't such a bad thing).

You can't grow up in the evangelical subculture and *not* compare yourself to those around you. I watched my friends get bombed on alcohol, saw girls in my church get pregnant and saw the cops show up at school to arrest my classmates, and I always knew I could fall back on the fact that no matter what I did, at least I wasn't as bad as *those* people. So I became comfortable with the notion that God must like me more than others because I was such a good kid.

But Moses' story blows several holes through that theory, as do the stories of many other major characters in the Bible. Are you telling me that God couldn't have found some other more stable personality to lead His people out of bondage? Perhaps the most wonderful aspect of God as shown through this story is His total disregard for *who you are* at this moment and His total belief in *who you will become* through friendship with Him. He destroys our notions of who is deserving and who isn't, because He knows our hearts and minds better than we do.

The Burning Bush

An interesting facet of Moses' story is the fact that when he flees from Pharaoh's home to save his neck, God leaves him to his own devices for a very long time. Moses finds a wife, makes a family, starts a job and probably figures he will simply live a normal life of no real consequence. I wonder how many nights he stared at the stars and thought about what "could have been" had he kept his wits about him and not gone postal on that guy. I'll bet he had more than a few sleepless nights thinking about it.

But when it is time to call Moses into his destiny, God once again reveals a portion of His character through the way He approaches Moses.

The Sunday school version of the burning bush that I grew up with is pretty much the way things go down. Moses is tending the flocks and sees a burning bush, out of which a voice speaks to him and points him to his destiny. But if you go back and reread the story, you can't help but notice a few things that weren't ever talked about.

> Now Moses was tending the flock of Jethro his father-in-law, the priest of Midian. And he led the flock to the back of the desert, and came to Horeb, the mountain of God. And the Angel of the LORD appeared to him in a flame of fire from the midst of a bush. So he looked, and behold, the bush was burning with fire, but the bush was not consumed. Then Moses said, "I will now turn aside and see this great sight, why the bush does not burn." So when the LORD saw that he turned aside to look, God called to him from the midst of the bush, and said, "Moses, Moses!" And he said, "Here I am."
>
> Exodus 3:1–4

This is the moment of truth for Moses. He doesn't know it yet, but he is about to have an encounter with God that will redirect his life and pull him not only into his destiny, but also into one of the greatest destinies in all of recorded history. For those of us still waiting for our own destinies to unfold or for dreams to be realized or for the desires of our hearts to become reality, much can be learned from this simple moment between God and an unsuspecting man.

The first thing I find strange about this episode (and honestly, I *always* thought it was strange) is the whole idea of a burning bush to begin with. Once again, God had an infinite amount of possibilities to work with here. He could have shown up in person as the "Angel of the Lord." He could have sent a regular angel. He could have blasted Moses with a bright light (á la Saul/Paul). He could have made one of Moses' sheep talk to him. The possibilities to freak Moses out were endless. Instead, He chose a burning bush. Why? Why choose an everyday object, set it on fire and not let the fire consume the bush? Why didn't He just use a flame of fire, which He would do later on when He was leading the Israelites through the desert? What's going on here?

I'm assuming that smarter people have posed this question and given way smarter answers than I'm about to give. If they have, then by all means go with what they say. But as I ponder this moment, I wonder if maybe God wanted to make Moses work for his encounter a little bit.

When I filmed in Israel for my movie *Father of Lights*, I walked around the wilderness that Moses was in, and I can tell you, it's a wild, somewhat barren place, and the sun is bright and hot. I don't think it's beyond reason to think that a bush that is on fire *from within*, meaning the flames weren't necessarily engulfing the whole bush, would be difficult to see. Sure, you'd be able to see it, but you'd have to be paying attention to your surroundings, and you'd have to be focused enough to realize that a particular bush over there looks a bit different from the bushes over here. Keep in mind, too, that if the fire was not consuming the bush, there would be no smoke.

If this is true, then it possibly explains why God didn't do something a little more overt. Maybe He wanted to see if Moses was paying attention. I have made no bones about my own stupidity when it came to things of God back before I started making *Finger of God*. I believed in God, went to church and did what I was supposed to do, but I wasn't really paying much attention to Him. I'm certain He put things in my path that called me into deeper understanding and relationship with Him that I either missed or ignored. The truth was, I didn't want to see any burning bushes, because that would mean I'd probably have to get out of my comfort zone and investigate, which could lead to a serious lifestyle change, which would have seriously cramped my style. Better to ignore the heavenly pokes and prods and just watch TV and play video games. No need to stir the pot when you're perfectly content.

The next statement furthers this idea, when God tells us what Moses was thinking: *I will now turn aside and see this great sight*. Obviously, this burning bush was not right in front of Moses, otherwise he wouldn't have to "turn aside" to see it. We'll probably never know how far away it was, but it's easy enough to see that Moses had to get off the path he was currently walking on to approach God. How often do we wonder why our lives are not panning out the way we want, or our destinies seem to be taking way too long to come to fruition, yet we have no intention of veering off the path we have chosen for ourselves?

As I have mentioned, I never, not in a million years, thought I was going to be a filmmaker. But then I had an encounter with an angel who told me to make the movie I knew God was calling me to, and if I wanted to step into my destiny I was going to have to veer off the path I was traveling. I was a professor, yes, but of *writing*. At the time I started *Finger of God*, I was teaching freshmen how to write term papers; I was not teaching them how to make movies. If I was going to do this thing God was asking me to do, I was going to have to step into territory I did not feel comfortable with. Of course, God was not calling me to do something *completely* out of my area of expertise. I did, after all, go to film school and study film structure and screenwriting, so I had some grid for what I was being asked to do. But picking up a camera and traveling the world and doing interviews? I hadn't done that. Ever.

With Moses, God is showing how He prefers to do things. He plants Himself by the side of the road and hopes that Moses will be paying enough attention to notice Him. It reminds me of my dog, who, coincidentally, is named Moses. In my opinion, this is the greatest dog who ever lived. The main reason I think this is because there is no doubt whatsoever that this dog is completely and madly in love with me. Wherever I go, he is there, always looking up at me, always attentive to my movements and my desires. If I want to pet him, I simply slap my legs and up he comes. If I want him to follow me, I stand up, walk a few paces, then nod my head, and he's right on my heels. I know he loves me because he's always paying attention to me and what I want.

When I was running from God, I would have told you I loved Him, but I was not the least bit interested in Him. I paid little attention to Him. When my wife and I have our seasons of "distance," it usually means doing our own thing and not paying much attention to each other; two ships passing in the night. So it wouldn't surprise me if God, who is love personified and desires above all else a loving relationship with us, is looking for lovers who will be wholly attentive to Him, even as He is wholly attentive to us. Too often with Him, though, the relationship is a one-way street. He meets our needs and ministers to us, and we completely ignore Him unless we need something from Him.

So when Moses notices this burning bush and turns from his path to investigate, you can almost sense God's heart skipping a beat. There is a curious moment in this story, when God writes: "When the LORD saw that he turned aside to look, God called to him . . . and said, 'Moses, Moses!'"

Here, God reveals even more of Himself. God does not call to Moses while he is on his own path, but instead waits until Moses decides to leave his path to approach Him. When we approach God, He speaks to us. Plain and simple. Love is a two-way street, and for our relationship with Him to thrive, there has to be some effort on our part to foster that relationship. Obviously, God is always desirous of us, always beckoning us with His fiery love, but this life with God is supposed to be a romantic dance of sorts. If He just keeps grabbing at us regardless of our response to Him, then He's just a creepy deity who's only in this for Himself. Instead, He is the consummate gentleman. When we show interest in Him, He takes a step closer to us.

God is waiting for us to respond to Him. I can think of no better example of this than my own experience. When I speak in churches, I often make light of the fact that I'm pretty sure I wasn't God's first choice to make the movies I currently make. I say this because over the years I have received at least fifteen different email messages from people around the world—professional filmmakers, men or women who own their own production companies, professional photographers (all people who are way more talented with a camera than I am)—and they all say the same thing.

Years ago, they felt God's call to travel the world and make a film about God's miraculous power, but for whatever reason (financial, time, fear, etc.) they either put the idea on hold or rejected it altogether as crazy, and then they looked up and saw that I had gone and done the very thing God had been calling them to do. Me, with my borrowed camera and $20,000 budget. So I have proof that I was, at minimum, God's sixteenth choice to make these movies. *Finger of God* probably would have been a way better movie had one of those people done it, but God works with whoever is willing. I then tell those churches that the only reason I'm standing here right now talking to them is because I'm the one guy who said yes.

I wonder if Moses is Moses simply because he said yes. I wonder if there were other guys tending their flocks, or outlaws on the run, who passed by the burning bush and either ignored it or weren't paying enough attention to notice it. It might be a stretch, and maybe Moses really was the only man for this particular job, but it certainly wouldn't surprise me if he was, like, number eight on God's wish list.

What Friendship Looks Like

When it was time for Moses to move into his destiny, God had a little bit of work to do to get His new friend's mind right. Exodus 4 tells the story of God giving Moses his marching orders, and Moses turning right around and trying to back out of his own calling. I'm sure you know the basics of the story. God directs Moses to go to Pharaoh and tell him to let the Israelites go, and Moses gives excuse after excuse as to why he could never do such a thing.

At first, God is patient with him and treats him gently, answering his questions and showing him a few miracles so he can kind of get his mind around this whole "God of the impossible" business. But after a while, Moses just gets plain irritating to God.

> "Oh, my Lord, please send someone else." Then the anger of the LORD was kindled against Moses and he said, "Is there not Aaron, your brother, the Levite? I know that he can speak well. Behold, he is coming out to meet you, and when he sees you, he will be glad in his heart. You shall speak to him and put the words in his mouth, and I will be with your mouth and with his mouth and will teach you both what to do. He shall speak for you to the people, and he shall be your mouth, and you shall be as God to him. And take in your hand this staff, with which you shall do the signs."
>
> Exodus 4:13–17 ESV

I love this scene, because it doesn't make me feel like such a numbskull for my own fear and trembling to step into whatever God is calling me to. When Moses has exhausted his excuses, he basically plops down in the dirt, crosses his arms and says, "But I don't want to do this! Pick somebody else."

Let's stop here and ponder a minute, shall we? Think about what Moses just experienced. He saw a burning bush that talked to him. He watched a stick turn into a snake and back into a stick again. He watched his hand instantly turn white with leprosy, then just as quickly go back to normal. Those are three pretty amazing things. I've heard my fair share of crazy God miracles, but I have to admit, I've never yet heard of a stick turning into a snake, then turning back into a stick. If I included that in one of my movies, I'd surely be accused of some hardcore CGI trickery. But for Moses, good old Moses, that was not enough for him. He was grasping at straws to get out of this assignment.

What was his problem? Shouldn't that be enough for Moses to say, "Hmm. You know what? I'm not seeing how this is all going to play out, but that was pretty darn impressive. If that's just a little parlor trick for You, God, then I'm all in to see what's going to happen when You pull out the big guns." But his response reveals much about human nature.

Our destinies are tricky things, because they are rooted in God's desires for us based on what He knows about us—and that just so happens to be knowledge that we typically aren't privy to yet. We see ourselves as grumpy, scared, untalented screw-ups, yet He sees something else entirely. He sees the leader. The visionary. The minstrel. But again, a relationship is only as strong as the level of trust between two people, and Moses is here showing what most who have been called into their destinies show: total distrust that God can handle it.

Moses can't see beyond his own limitations. It is these limitations that keep him from moving forward, that keep giving him more and more excuses to throw back at God. You get the sense that this conversation could have gone on for quite some time.

But then, God has had enough. He has work to do. People are crying out for Him to save them, and this kid of His is refusing to move because he can't see what God sees. So His anger kindles against Moses, which, honestly, probably scared the living daylights out of the poor guy. Notice after God goes off on him, Moses doesn't object anymore. I don't think any of us would.

But how often do we do this ourselves? We feel the tug of God in our hearts or we receive a prophetic word or we feel that God is speaking to us about doing something, but when we look at it practically, it makes no sense because we are in no way capable of doing such a thing. So we hem and we haw, and we create a lot of really good excuses that obviously God didn't think about when He so rashly called us to do this thing, and we breathe a sigh of relief that we, thankfully, saw the flaws in God's plan before it was too late. These days, thanks to Jesus' sacrifice, God's anger isn't kindled against our excuses. It's actually much worse than that. He just moves on to the next person, hoping he or she will say yes to Him.

I am constantly meeting people who are frustrated because they feel they have a destiny, and they've received, like, 24 prophetic words all about the same thing, and they don't understand why nothing is happening in this area. But, of course, they aren't actually *doing* anything to move forward;

they simply keep waiting for one more word, one more sign, one more instruction telling them that now is the time to do it. All the while they have forgotten that if God has given the word, He has already provided the way. We just can't see it because our limitations blind us.

This picture of Moses is important to note when we compare it to the man he is going to become later in Exodus. God was indeed right about him. As we see later, when Moses becomes comfortable with his true identity as God's beloved friend, he speaks to Pharaoh and the Israelites without the aid of Aaron. God was right about him after all. Big shocker.

Compare this fearful, trembling man to the one we see in Exodus 32. This is the whole golden calf fiasco. While God and Moses have been hanging out on the mountain together, the Israelites have set up a statue factory down at base camp. God tells Moses in verse 7: "Go, get down! For your people whom you brought out of the land of Egypt have corrupted themselves." I love this. God is so angry that he does the old parenting move I sometimes use with my wife when our kids have been particularly irritating—the old "Go deal with your son" ploy. Right now, God is hot. He tells Moses that He knows these people (of course, He does), and you can almost see Him pushing Moses aside as He gets ready to obliterate the whole lot of them. He then shows His sheer pleasure in Moses when He says, "Now therefore, let Me alone, that My wrath may burn hot against them and I may consume them. And I will make of you a great nation" (Exodus 32:10).

But then Moses does something that only a friend can do.

Have you ever been so angry that you almost can't think clearly? You're about to pop, and consequences be damned. You're not thinking about consequences; you're in a rage. What if, at that moment, a casual acquaintance approaches you and tells you to cool off? Chances are you'd pop him in the mouth, then move on to the thing that really had you steamed. The only person who can speak to you in those moments of passionate anger is someone you trust implicitly, someone who loves you and wants the best for you. Someone who understands your pain and anger, but who has also gone through the fire with you. Now if *that* person steps in and tells you to cool off, chances are you're at least going to listen. The fact that God was about to go nuclear on the very people He chose for Himself, and that Moses was able to calm Him down should tell you all you need to know about the level of their friendship at this point.

Moses is given an amazing offer here; don't forget that. An entirely new nation could be built with him as the cornerstone. That's pretty heady stuff, and it shows his true mettle that he declines the offer. It is also further testament to what God saw in this murderer in the first place.

Moses, in essence, changes God's mind. The next time you don't think your prayers mean a hill of beans, go back and read this story. One man speaks to God, and God changes the whole course of human history. This is the level of friendship God is looking for with you. If that doesn't get your blood pumping, I'm not sure what will.

Perhaps the greatest individual event I ever filmed was the miracle of me getting into the Dome of the Rock. Let me tell you how it all happened, as it speaks to this very idea we are discussing.

The Miracle of the Dome

Even before I began filming *Father of Lights*, I knew that it
had to end in Israel. I had no idea why, other than something
cryptic I felt the Lord was telling me when He first put it on
my heart: *It all ends in Israel. It must end where it all began.*
That's pretty much what I had to go on for the next year,
but it was at least enough to point me in the right direction.

When I was out in Redding, California, at Bethel Church
for the opening of *Furious Love* in 2010, I met Todd White for
the first time. I had heard of him and even seen a few short
videos of him praying for people on the streets, so I knew
enough about him to know that our paths would likely cross
at some point. But he was doing his thing and I was doing
mine, and that's pretty much where I figured it would stay.
I had no real desire to film with him, honestly. But then we
were introduced to each other by our mutual friend, Robby
Dawkins, and I received the full Todd White love experience.

Here is pretty much all you need to know about Todd. For
most of his life he was a despicable human being—a drug
addict, violent and completely self-absorbed. Then one day,
during a drug deal, he tried to rip off a teenage kid for some
crack cocaine, and the kid unloaded six bullets through his
car window as Todd stepped on the gas and drove away. None
of the bullets touched him. While Todd's adrenaline was
calming down and he realized what had just happened, he
heard an audible voice say, *I took those bullets for you; now
will you live for Me?*

This led Todd straight into the arms of Jesus, and the guy
honestly hasn't been the same (or completely normal) since.
He picked up the Bible and started reading it. Since he had

no upbringing in the church, he took the Bible literally and figured that if Jesus told people to go pray for the sick, then that's what every Christian was supposed to do. So he started praying for everyone in need he came across, and kept a record of each encounter. Over a six-month period, Todd prayed for more than seven hundred people and didn't see one miracle. Not one. But he was determined that Jesus wasn't lying, so he kept going after it, over and over and over again. Eventually he saw his first miracle. Obviously, he's seen a few more since then.

I didn't know this part of Todd's story when I first met him. All I knew was that he was a cool-looking guy with big-time dreadlocks, and that he had a reputation for being fairly radical. After about five minutes with him, I knew he was different from most. For one thing, he kept telling me that he loved me. And he couldn't stop talking about how much he loved Jesus. It was just love, love, love, all the time, nonstop. But it was so sincere it even started to melt my jaded, cynical heart. That's about the time God spoke to me.

Take him to Israel.

Keep in mind, I had just begun to *think* about *Father of Lights*. I didn't have much planned yet. All I knew was that it ended in Israel, and my first trip was going to be to Russia.

Todd kept rattling on about how he just wants to be love to others, and I had a hard time following him, because that little voice in my head was nonstop: *Take him to Israel. Take him to Israel. Take him to Israel.* So finally I just blurted, "Hey, dude, would you be interested in going with me to film in Israel?" He said, "Absolutely," and that was it.

Todd and I kept in touch throughout the process of my filming. He was in town during our time with the Latin King gang leaders, so I was able to see him minister firsthand there. His whole message was God's grace, so I knew he would be a perfect fit at least for the message of the film. But it wasn't until we actually got to Israel that I realized why this guy was perhaps the best person on the planet for this particular assignment in Israel.

The God of the Impossible

The day before we left for Israel, I sat in my studio and prayed. I normally do this before I go anywhere, as it's kind of my last moment of clarity and sanity before I head off toward my next destination. Typically, once I get on the plane to wherever, my mind is going a hundred miles an hour, and while I'm listening to hear what God wants, it's somehow different. It's more hectic, more off the cuff, more in the moment. I like to contemplate what I'm about to do before I go, so I can have an intelligent conversation with the Lord before the craziness starts and all my best laid plans are (usually) laid to waste.

This particular time of prayer was especially charged. I knew two things going in: (1) God wanted me to go there with Todd; and (2) this was the end. I already knew that *Father of Lights* was the end of a long journey, and that when I finished this trilogy I would be moving on to films that had a different feel, a different style, and were, essentially, a different journey for me. I'd make many more movies, for sure, but this particular journey was about to come to a close. So I sat on my chair in my studio and had a fairly intense heart-to-heart with the Lord.

"God," I prayed, "this is the end, You know. The end of it all. This whole journey has been so big and epic and has touched so many lives, we've got to go out with a bang. You've got to do something totally impossible; something nobody can ever accuse me of setting up or staging. Will You please do something in Israel that will blow everybody's mind who sees it? Please allow me to film something impossible."

This was my prayer, and although I had no idea what God was going to do, I knew that something about this trip felt different. I had come full circle in my faith since I had started *Finger of God* as a reluctant skeptic, and now I had full and utter confidence that God was going to come through. I'd seen enough. It was as if I had finished Faith School, and this was going to be my coronation ceremony. I knew He was going to come through. I just knew it.

Of course, *what* He was going to do was another question. I certainly had my own ideas as far as what it should be. I didn't come right out and ask for this, but God, who knows me better than I know myself, knew exactly what I was hoping for. I wanted to film a resurrection from the dead. In Israel. Yeah, that would do.

So we headed to Israel, looking for something impossible, and as soon as we got there God was moving full force. Our first miracles took place in the car rental area just after we landed. The whole rental place was rocked by God's love and in a general state of shock as each person got touched. That's all it took for me to know that this trip was going to be special, and that Todd was the right man for the job.

We only had five days in Israel, one of our shortest trips ever. So everything was compacted. Everywhere we went we were on the lookout for something God might want to do. Todd was fearless. He prayed, prophesied and loved on literally everyone he met, I've never seen anything quite like it. People just responded to him, and, by our unofficial count, of the 47 people he prayed for in those five days, 43 were totally healed. It was nuts.

Even though God was moving, I knew I still didn't have my ending. I had shared with Todd on the plane that I was asking God for something impossible, and he was game for whatever might come up. So together we kept an eye out for impossible things. At one point he prayed for a man with no eyeballs, and I wondered if I was about to film eyeballs appearing out of thin air. That would be pretty impossible. But nothing happened, so the guy at least got a big hug out of it and the knowledge that God loved him.

We were staying with a beautiful couple named Gary and Cindy Beyer, and Gary was one of the greatest tour guides I've ever met. He knew everything about everywhere. At one point, we were sitting in his living room, I think, and I was rifling through a guidebook on Israel. I turned to a page on the Dome of the Rock. I had seen that golden dome many times in pictures of Jerusalem, but I have to admit I knew very little about it. So as I read, I noticed that the dome was built on the second holiest site in Islam, as well as the place where Abraham almost sacrificed Isaac, and the location where the Jewish Tabernacle and later Solomon's Temple, both of which housed the Ark of the Covenant, once stood. This was obviously some prime real estate. Then I read the sentence that changed everything.

"Since 2003, non-Muslims have not been allowed inside."

This piqued my interest, so I asked Gary about it. He gave me a little more history on the place, and I asked him how I might be able to get inside to film.

"Oh," he said with a smile. "It's impossible. You'd never get in."

My head snapped toward Todd, and his to mine. We both smiled. He had just said the magic word.

"Well, then, that's where I want to go."

Gary literally laughed at me. He was good-natured, but it was obvious that he believed that under no circumstances would we ever get into that place.

"Guys, you have to understand, you're allowed to be on the Temple Mount, which is the area around the Dome, but during the call to prayer, they even kick all non-Muslims off of *that*. You're not getting in there."

We were leaving for Jerusalem the next day.

"We'll see," I said.

That night I posted on Facebook for the world to be praying for us because we were going to attempt the impossible. The next morning, I found that my post had gone viral; it was spreading across Facebook and Twitter like wildfire. So at least we had a lot of people praying for us.

We headed down to Jerusalem. Along the way we stopped at the Jordan River to see where Jesus was baptized. We were in no hurry, because, well, what were we going to do? We had no plan, we weren't going to meet anyone there. So we hung around for a bit, explored an abandoned building, and basically took our sweet time getting to Jerusalem from Galilee.

If you've seen *Father of Lights*, you know the rest. If you haven't seen it, I don't want to ruin the surprise. Needless to say, through one of the most supernatural and miraculous encounters I've ever heard of, let alone filmed, we got into the Dome. I remember Gary's reaction when we called him to tell him what had happened. He could not believe it, and he openly repented for his lack of faith. He'd seen a lot in his day, he admitted, but never anything like that.

The point of all this is simple. God did the impossible for me because I asked Him to. End of story. Trust must be built up between friends, and my trust level when I started *Finger of God* was nil. I was as curious as the next guy to see if God was going to do *anything* when I went out to film. But by the time I was at the end of *Father of Lights*, I had seen too much to doubt Him. I had seen Him come through time and again when I turned on that camera—I had seen the fruit from our times filming together—and I knew that He wanted a great ending just as much as I did.

I also knew that at this point He trusted me. I had proven myself to Him, proven that I could be trusted with endeavoring to capture His greatness on film. So I knew that I could ask Him for the impossible and that He would give me something impossible. Obviously there was some level of doubt; there always is. But for the first time in my life, my level of faith outweighed my level of doubt. Everyone said it was impossible, but God is the God of the impossible.

The Responsibility of Friendship

When you become true friends with someone, it means you have moved to another level together, and certain expectations go along with that deeper bond. Moses is no different.

Since I've always had a fondness for Moses, I could never understand the harshness of his punishment the one time he screwed up. It seemed totally unfair to me and more than a little petty. But the more I began to understand friendship with God, the more I understood the dynamics of what happened between him and God at that rock.

In Exodus 17, we see the first story of Moses drawing water from a rock. The Israelites are stuck in the desert with no water and begin to riot against Moses. You can sense an uprising beginning that is not going to end well for our man Moses. So he complains to God to do something, and the Lord, ever patient, tells him to go to a rock and strike it with his staff, and God will make water pour forth from it. And, of course, that's exactly what happens. Awesome story, and way stranger than anything I've ever filmed!

Then we have a kind of repeat of this desert event later in Numbers 20:8–13. The people again start complaining about water, and Moses goes to the Lord to inquire what to do. God tells him and Aaron to gather the congregation together: "Speak to the rock . . . and it will yield its water." God will take it from there. Moses gathers the people and gets a little too theatrical for his own good. He proclaims, "Must we bring water for you out of this rock?" He then strikes it twice with his staff, and it brings forth water. This, in turn, ticks God off something terrible, and He tells Moses he can forget about going into the Promised Land.

As I said, this story always bothered me for a couple of reasons. The first, most obvious one for me was why God allowed water to come from the rock at all. Moses stood up there, made a big show of himself and hit the rock with his staff. It isn't as though he was some magician with superpowers. All miracles come from God; therefore, God was not at all obligated to do what Moses wanted. If what Moses was doing was wrong, why didn't God just let the staff hit the rock and nothing happen? Moses would look like an idiot, and the people would be reminded who was really in charge. Seems simple enough to me.

But this, again, shows the character of God. Even in our rebellion, He loves us. Even in the middle of our stupidity, when we are directly disobeying Him, He extends His hand of mercy and grace to us. That doesn't mean there won't be consequences (for Moses, the consequences were severe), but at that moment, God showed that His ties to friendship are greater than His ties to judgment. His friend was making a mistake, a pretty big one as we'll soon see, but this was still His friend, and, therefore, God gave him what he was asking for. God's grace never ceases to astound me.

My next, and much bigger question, regards the aftermath of this episode. Okay, I get that Moses didn't technically do what God asked, but does that negate everything else Moses had gone through, everything else he had done as the Father's mouthpiece? All his sacrifice, all his stepping out in faith, all of his good and faithful work on the Lord's behalf—was it completely negated because Moses struck the rock as opposed to speaking to it? It just doesn't seem fair.

The easy view of this would be that God has high standards for His friends; those to whom much is given, much is expected. If you have that kind of intimacy with God where He speaks and shows Himself openly to you, it would behoove you to do exactly as He says all the time. He is the boss, after all.

But that only partially explains it, I think. What is really going on here speaks more to the level of intimacy involved

in being God's best friend. Moses was not simply disobeying directions; he was exalting himself. The Bible speaks of
Moses as the most humble man in the world (see Numbers
12:3), but he was anything but humble here. He was trying
to make a point. He was upset and frustrated, and he wanted
to reestablish his authority over these people. "Do we have
to bring forth water from this rock for you?" In other words,
it was not God who would be doing this, but Moses. This is
pride, pure and simple. The position went to his head, and
we see a crack in his armor.

If you are going to walk this closely with God, you had
better know your place in the pecking order. Sometimes we
get a little *too* comfortable with God. His love is so over-
powering, we start to view Him more as a passive lover than
the fiery God of the universe. He is the King, and we must
treat Him as such. He just happens to be a King who invites
us up to His throne for a hug. But it is still *His* throne, and
we cannot for a second think that we can reside there any
longer than He wishes us to.

God's punishment for Moses is actually an act of mercy.
It is not the cold-hearted, petty punishment of a ruler who
is annoyed; it is grace and mercy through and through.

Moses had come to a place of extreme intimacy with the
Lord, and, for God, intimacy with His kids is of primary
importance. He will do anything to keep that, even if it means
stopping our ministry or keeping us from reaching others.
Jesus tells us that the Father will leave 99 sheep on their own
to go find the one that has wandered off. If we wander off
from Him in pursuit of our own glory, that directly affects
our ability to walk in intimacy with Him, and He will actually

go so far as to abandon others to get us back. His passion for us is not to be trifled with.

In Moses' case, this is the first sign that he is beginning to wander off; he starts believing his own press clippings. God is in danger of losing His best friend, and He is *not* going to let that happen. So He brings down the greatest punishment of all to Moses, one that he will certainly think about every day for the rest of his life. Where he is leading these people, he will not be able to enter.

I say this is an act of mercy because it will be a constant reminder for Moses to know his place, to keep his pride in check, and, therefore, keep his relationship with God intact. I'm sure this is a bitter pill for Moses to swallow, but I'm equally sure that the alternative would be far more devastating to him. Moses says as much when, at one point, he pleads with God not to abandon the people, as moving into the Promised Land without Him would be pointless. God is everything to Moses, and now, as Moses is poised to career out of control, God reminds him of what it is going to take to remain in that place of intimacy.

But of course, God is, deep down, a giant softy. And this is His good friend, after all. His desire is to give us good things all the time—it is His greatest joy. All good things come down from the Father of Lights; goodness is His very nature.

Jump forward a few thousand years to Matthew 17, where Jesus takes Peter, James and John up the mountain for His Transfiguration. Whom do we find meeting Him there but Elijah and Moses? The Lord lets him into the Promised Land after all. And as the ultimate bonus prize of all time, he not only enters the Promised Land, but he gets to meet with Jesus when he does! It's just like God to give us our heart's desire, and at the same time show us what our *real* heart's desire is while He's doing it.

Mercy. Grace. Goodness. This is the very heart of God.

Fighting for a Dead Body

The last story I want to highlight in Moses' saga is perhaps one of the strangest. The book of Jude says this: "Yet Michael the archangel, in contending with the devil, when he disputed about the body of Moses, dared not bring against him a reviling accusation, but said, 'The Lord rebuke you!'" (Jude 1:9).

While this verse is making the point about something else (speaking evil of others), you can't help but wonder at the example given! Michael and Lucifer battle over Moses' dead body? What's up with that?

The question is obvious: What would the devil want with Moses' dead body? While this is pure conjecture, consider that Moses was God's best friend, and the devil knows he meant a great deal to the Father; therefore, since the devil couldn't touch Moses in his lifetime, he'd touch him in death. I picture those horrific scenes we used to see on the news when dead American soldiers were dragged through the streets of Iraq behind cars as a sign of contempt for both the soldier and the one who sent the soldier. Moses caused so much damage to the kingdom of darkness you can only presume that the devil, in his bloodthirsty rage, wanted to destroy the corpse in the worst way imaginable. It would be like giving a satanic middle finger to God.

But this is God's friend we're talking about. And just as we would never leave a friend who has died lying by the side of the road, but would go out of our way to bury him as a sign of respect for our friendship, so God sent His top general to take care of business and keep Moses' body safe from harm.

Still, this is a corpse. The life has gone out of it; it is merely rotting flesh. What does it matter what happens to that flesh?

God has feelings, just as we have feelings, and His feelings for His friend shine through in this story. If He cares this much for the dead body of His friend, how much more must He care about our living ones!

Ultimately, we know how this story ends—as revealed in Deuteronomy 34:6: God Himself buries Moses' body in a secret place known only to Him. It is a fitting end to a life rooted in friendship. Michael obviously wins the battle for the body, and God then takes it, alone, and buries it properly. It is a solitary act, and one that points to the truly wonderful nature of God. He deals with us individually. He attends to us individually. He loves us individually. He feels for us individually. He cares for us individually.

Somewhere on the plains of Moab in Israel, there comes a moment when the God who created the entire universe is alone with a body of a man, the spirit having left, and only flesh and bones remaining. God digs into the dirt with His own hands and lays the corpse into the ground, then covers it Himself. There are no witnesses to this event, because this is not for anyone else but God. It is God attending to the body of His best friend. And it is an extraordinary thing indeed.

6

And You Think Your Family Is a Bunch of Jerks!

As far as pure story is concerned, it's hard to find a better one in the Bible than that of Joseph. This narrative, played out over decades, includes sibling rivalry of epic proportions, prophetic dreams, false accusations and the near collapse of one of the greatest nations in human history. In the end, though, it is a story of redemption through the goodness and faithfulness of God. Along the way we learn quite a bit more about His character.

God's Big Dreams

I've always had a bit of a soft spot for Joseph. How can you not? The guy comes off as one of the most honest men in the

Bible (as opposed to his father, Jacob). But at the same time, I can't help but think that if he had had just a little more social awareness he could have saved himself a lifetime of trouble.

We first meet Joseph as a seventeen-year-old. Immediately we see a kid who doesn't know when to keep his mouth shut, even though he speaks the truth. His brothers already hate him, which you figure he had to know. You get the sense that, even now, Joseph is kind of a loner, an outcast because of jealousy. You wonder in the days of early Palestine if this poor kid has any friends at all. But here he is, telling his hostile brothers about a dream he had in which they bow down and worship him. Twice! Even his father, in whose eyes Joseph can do no wrong, "rebukes" him for his dream. Jacob did, to his credit, store this episode away in his heart.

It is interesting that God even gave Joseph these dreams. Obviously He knew the family dynamics and how tenuous it all was, so one can only surmise that God was knocking over the first domino that would ultimately lead Joseph to the throne in Egypt; it would have to get much worse before it got better for poor Joseph. But I also think there is something gracious in these dreams. Joseph didn't receive just one, but two separate dreams showing him his destiny. Lest there be any doubt that God was with Joseph, especially considering what was coming for him, perhaps these would be enough to carry him through.

Jacob, of course, didn't do Joseph any favors. Joseph was the supreme favorite of his father, and choosing favorites among your kids is never a good parenting choice. You can sense the broiling hostility as the family sits around the fire, and Joseph gets the choicest piece of meat or gets served first.

Then, when his father goes out of his way to create a beautiful coat for his favorite son, it is simply too much for the others to bear. It is unfortunate that they take their anger out on their brother as opposed to their father, who was actually the one fueling their hatred, but our anger toward others is often misguided like this. When Joseph tattles on his brothers, the picture of total family dysfunction is complete.

The rest of the story should be familiar to anyone who spent even a day in Sunday school. Joseph is sent to check on his brothers who are tending the flock, and, as he approaches, God writes that his brothers plot to kill him. Now I've seen a good many family squabbles in my day, but none that got to this point. The hatred must have been unbearable for these boys to sink to this level of evil. It is bad enough to plot to kill anyone, let alone your own brother. But there is something in this story that piques my interest, something that reveals why they never went through with their plan.

Genesis 37:19–20 mentions the idea of killing Joseph, but it also reveals their motive. Those dreams pushed them over the top. It was awful to have to watch their father love him more than them, but it was simply too much to consider the idea of bowing to him. We don't know who said it, but someone spoke for the whole group: "We shall see what will become of his dreams!"

And with that, the brothers stepped onto one of the worst land mines known to man. God gave Joseph those dreams; therefore, this was God's plan for his life. His brothers were about to destroy God's plan, and that is a place I suggest you try to stay away from. We may disregard our own dreams, peddling them off as fancy or wishful thinking, and we may (and often do) put them off so long that they become distant memory at best or bitter regret at worst. Sometimes we consider our own dreams childish or foolish or unrealistic. Whatever we do with them, the common denominator for a frightfully large number of people is that our dreams for ourselves are simply not that important.

But God's dreams, those are a different story altogether. The dreams our good Father has for His children are potent, laced with promise and, above all, deadly serious. My children may one day say they don't deserve to be happy based on some horrible, misguided theology that poisons them, but as their father, I will never even think such a thought. My goal is to raise them well, teach them right from wrong, love them always no matter what and hope they are happy in whatever they choose to do.

In the same way, the Father dreams for us. Due to our own distractions or immaturity or unwillingness to yield to Him, though, often those dreams never get communicated to us. We are simply not ready for them. Some people are so wrapped up in their own issues, bitterness, hurts or careers that they will never be ready to hear the whispers of a good Father trying to guide them. But sometimes, when our decisions are sound and our character has begun to meet with His approval, He will open our eyes to what He has in store for us—His dreams for us. For Joseph, God showed him His dreams in, well, his dreams.

So when Joseph's brothers plot against him and talk of killing him, this is in direct opposition to what the Father has in store for Joseph. These dreams are more than mere happiness for Joseph, as almost all of God's ideas and plans are. He's a multi-purposer, our Father, and He wishes Joseph not only a destiny of greatness, but one that will literally save millions of people from starvation.

Reuben stands up for his little brother, albeit weakly. Reuben is the oldest and, therefore, we assume the most mature. He senses that the hatred has gone far enough. He plans to go along with a terrible prank, but believes he will ultimately pull Joseph out of the pit. One has to believe he hopes it will knock some sense into his little brother as well.

Was It God's Fault?

This is where the story of Joseph gets quite dark. We would do well to pause here and ponder the full extent of his anguish as his entire life comes crashing down around him. Genesis 37:23–25 says that the brothers strip Joseph of his tunic and throw him into a dry cistern, after which they sit down and eat lunch. Genesis 42:21 fills out the picture, when the brothers stand before an older Joseph in Egypt and agree among themselves that they are being punished because of what they did to their brother. Obviously, these men carry guilt for decades, as it is the first thing they bring up when calamity strikes them. Then they admit this: "We saw the anguish of his soul when he pleaded with us, and we would not hear. . . ."

What cruelty must it take to strip a person, throw him down a well shaft, then sit down and eat your lunch within earshot of his cries for mercy? Sounds like something the Nazis would do. Joseph is still young at this point, so his terror must be evident in his cracking voice. That this is their own flesh and blood is even worse. What must Joseph be thinking as he claws at the sides of the pit, screaming for his life—the chosen one now doomed by his own brothers?

Apparently it has some effect, as Judah decides that maybe this is a bad idea after all, and suggests they sell him instead. You know, because selling him into slavery is much more humane than simply killing him. All agree, and once again you can just imagine a seventeen-year-old boy crying, shouting to his brothers please not to do this, while they all stand there and coldly count their money. Reuben, for some reason, is absent when this happens, and is horrified to learn what his brothers have done when he returns to the cistern to fetch Joseph. But God's plan has just been put into motion.

We should pause here and consider another accusation that is often raised against the Father based on this story. I used to read this as simply one more example of why God is not to be trusted. If I surrender to Him, surely some hardship awaits me. Joseph's story carries with it a sense of inevitability, almost as if God is orchestrating all these turns of events to reach His desired outcome. Yet the more I learn of God's character, and the more I learn of man's character, the more I look upon this story through a different lens of understanding. There are two ways, in my opinion, to view the story of Joseph. God, who knows the end from the beginning, is either the aggressor who actually *causes* all these things to happen, or the reactionary who adjusts on the fly.

The first view is, I think, the most popular. At least it is the one I believed for most of my life. God causes Joseph's brothers to be jealous; causes them to sell him into slavery;

causes Potiphar to purchase him; causes Potiphar's wife to try to seduce and then accuse him; causes him to be thrown into jail; and so on and so forth. But this theory flies in the face of a good, loving, compassionate God who "tempts no man to sin." There is *much* sinning against Joseph, and if God tempts no man to sin, then it doesn't make sense that God is orchestrating all of this. It makes more sense, in my humble opinion, that He is simply reacting to the incredibly horrible and stupid decisions of all the major characters in this story.

We have no idea of the quickest way for Joseph to go from his father's table to the second most powerful seat in Egypt, but based on his dreams, we can be certain it was God's plan from the very beginning. Was there another, less arduous way for this to happen? It is possible that Joseph's character needed to be tested and honed in order to handle the power he was to be given, but I wonder if there were other methods God intended to use to do that sharpening.

I have traveled the world and seen many things while making my films, and one thing has become abundantly clear. The capacity for man to be evil is as astounding as it is boundless. Whether it's watching the forced servitude of entire families in the rock quarries of India, or the systematic raping of women for sport and pleasure in Thailand, we humans have an insatiable appetite for cruelty. My grandfather told, for instance, how as one of the first soldiers in World War II to liberate the concentration camps in Germany, he saw horrors that have never been reported in history books, because they were cleaned up before the press arrived. He walked into a building on the outskirts of Dachau, cloaked in thick woods, and saw the bodies of babies hanging from meat hooks through their jaws. Whatever drives men to such depravity and evil is one of the great questions of our day, and it is quickly followed by this: Why in the world would a loving God ever allow it?

Was God behind the concentration camps of Hitler? Were those His ideas, planted in the mind of a madman so that some cosmic purpose could be completed? To suggest such a thing only proves one's lack of understanding of a good and loving Father. I would never sacrifice one of my children for the sake of another, and our Father is no different.

Joseph's problems started because his earthly father made a mistake. Jacob favored him. This in turn flamed jealousy in his other children, and, of course, Joseph didn't do himself any favors with his raw honesty. Did God plant the idea for Joseph's brothers to kill him, or did He perhaps whisper a new plan of mercy? Their hearts were black as night to do what they did, and you can sense the Holy Spirit working overtime just to save the boy's neck from their villainy.

I never used to trust God because I always believed God directed my path with or without my consent. While I still believe that to a point, I also have a much more realistic view of free will than ever before. You can see only so much heartache and evil done to your fellow man before you realize that all of the heartache and evil in the world is the result of decisions made by *people*, not God. God has a plan for my life, a plan to prosper, but quite often other people get in the way of that plan. Quite often I get in the way of that plan. I've been called to reveal the Father's heart to as many people in the world as possible, but if I decide to pick up a gun and shoot someone in the head, that plan will come to a screeching halt because of *my* actions. And more importantly, the plan for the person I shot will come to a screeching halt, too.

Instead of seeing God in Joseph's story as a Puppeteer who is controlling everyone, I now see Him as One who works with what's available, however limited and meager that might be.

Genesis 39:2 tells us all we need to know about God's character and nature in this story. "The LORD was with Joseph, and he was a successful man." Now, I am as firmly set against the "prosperity gospel" as anyone you will meet, but there is no denying that God's desire *is* for us to prosper. If He is with us, we will prosper. Of course, what *prosper* means to us and to God is usually quite different. The real problem comes when we step outside of His will for us, step outside of relationship with Him and try to do things on our own.

I had thirty years of creative failure simply because I was chasing after my own dreams and desires. God used my failures to build my character as well as my craft, but I could have achieved more had I been seeking His direction. Even so, God was with me those thirty years, and I found favor in the sight of men because His favor was upon my life. I believe that God's favor rests on us all to a degree, but it kicks into high gear once we have the courage and faith to step into His call on our lives.

In Joseph's case, his destiny was forced upon him by his jerk brothers. But when God chooses to place His favor on your life, it's pretty tough to work your way out of that favor. So it was that Joseph just *happened* to be bought by Potiphar, and he *happened* to be successful at everything he did, which in turn caused Potiphar to *happen* to turn everything in his household over to him. Joseph became executor of

Potiphar's estate, which most likely was a plum job and one that Joseph figured he'd be doing for the rest of his life. But, as usual, God's plans for Joseph were much, much bigger than Joseph's own plans.

And this is one attribute of God I see time and again. God tipped His hand when He gave Joseph those dreams of others bowing down to him: *That* was God's dream for Joseph. It was also God's way to get this kid to start paying attention to his dreams and begin to examine them and work to understand them.

Training Grounds and Trust

So Joseph goes to work for Potiphar, who's a big shot in Egypt, and presumably has one heck of an estate to manage. Joseph runs this guy's household so competently that eventually all Potiphar has to worry about is what he will eat that day. How many of us are perfectly content to run our current state of affairs, even though we know we are called to something more? Quite often, our current affairs are the training ground for the greater affairs our Father has in mind for us. Joseph has to learn how to run a successful household so he can one day run a successful nation.

When my family learned that I was going to be a professor, the common response was laughter. It's not that they thought I wasn't smart enough; intelligence had nothing to do with my family's constant snickering. Instead, it was the fact that I was perhaps the worst public speaker they knew. I couldn't tell a joke to save my life. My speech was halting, my narratives rarely followed a fluid path, and I was uncomfortable speaking to groups. The only speech class I took in college yielded a C. I just couldn't get my thoughts in order in my head when I saw all those people looking at me.

But God saw His dreams for me way before I saw them myself. He saw me speaking in front of thousands of people around the world, saw me ministering to them, telling them stories about His greatness; therefore, He found a suitable training ground for me. I wasn't the greatest speaker in the world those first few years, not by a long shot, but I knew that I did not want to be a boring professor. So I tried out new things, new ways of communicating, and over time I not only grew to enjoy speaking in front of people, but actually became quite good at it. It was as if I had been born to do this, which, of course, I had!

One thing I've learned about God is that He's always about a thousand steps ahead of the curve. As my friend Greg Boyd likes to say, God has infinite intelligence. Just as a great chess player can think fifteen or twenty moves ahead based on his opponent's latest move, so God can think years ahead and examine every possible move each person you come in contact with might make. He obviously sees Potiphar's wife coming a mile away, and He knows that Joseph's time there is going to be fruitful but short. Sure enough, Joseph is falsely accused of attempting to rape Potiphar's wife, and is thrown into prison.

Then, of course, he meets the butler and the baker (and presumably the candlestick maker) and interprets their dreams for them. Joseph then has to wait another two years before Pharaoh has a dream no one can figure out, and he is called on to interpret. Obviously, God is in the business of using our dreams to speak to us, and it is a shame how little thought we often give to them.

But as interesting as it might be to linger on these dreams trying to figure out God's specific symbolisms therein, I am much more interested in Joseph's ultimate dreams, and specifically the amount of time it takes for them to be fulfilled.

Think about this. Joseph has spent *years* away from his father, *years* as a slave, and now he is spending *years* rotting in a prison for a crime he didn't commit. It stands to reason that he has many nights where he despairs of any hope that anything sustainably good will ever happen to him, or if he will instead die a lonely death in obscurity. We often find it difficult to trust God when times are tough because our minds are finite and small, and we can only see the immediate.

A good friend of mine was forced to suffer the loss of her brother and sister-in-law because they could not see past the immediate darkness in front of them. Newly married, this couple had suffered a miscarriage, and with it came all the grief and mental torment of losing a child. Brought to the breaking point, the young wife took a gun and shot herself in the head. For days she lingered on life support, and her husband, my friend's brother, prayed and begged for a miracle that never came. The decision was made to pull the plug, and this husband, drowning in unresolved grief, went back to his hotel room and hanged himself.

Two families had to bury their children together because the finite and fragile minds of humans sometimes cannot see the forest through the trees. This is especially difficult when you are the one suffering. Others can often see clearly on your behalf—my friend kept telling her brother that in time, although the scar would always remain, this wound in his heart would heal. But he couldn't see it, which caused him to make a terrible, tragic decision.

So I imagine Joseph sitting in prison—knowing he was innocent when his brothers sold him into slavery, knowing he was innocent in Potiphar's home—and I have to wonder if he has some pointed conversations with God.

But God sees the whole picture, and His trump card is that He can make the impossible possible. Joseph sees no way out in the immediate; but then God *gives* Pharaoh a dream that no one but Joseph can interpret, which frees an innocent man and elevates him to the second-most powerful position in the country.

We think we are so smart, but, in reality, we're little children compared to our Father. If I were to take my four-year-old son and hand him a pile of blocks and tell him to build a tower that reaches the ceiling, I realize that I am asking him to do something that he believes is impossible. Even if he stands on a chair, there's no way he can do it all the way. He then has to make a decision. Does he trust his dad and start building, believing that his father will provide a way for him to succeed? Or does he walk away, shaking his head at his silly father for asking such an impossible thing of him?

Most Christians, I think, shake their heads and walk away. Or they stand in the room, staring at the blocks, twiddling their fingers, waiting for something "magical" to happen to jump-start the process. Occasionally, though, someone takes his Father at His word, and, against all odds, begins assembling the blocks, one by one, until he has gone as high as he can go. Then his Father brings over a chair, and the child steps onto it and makes the tower higher, and still he realizes that he will never reach the goal without his Father's help.

And as soon as he has gone as far as he can go, and whatever he can do on his own has been accomplished, his Father knows that this child trusts Him completely. He firmly picks the little one up and puts him on His shoulders, and holds him tightly as he continues to build the tower, block by block. The child's mind could not foresee that his Father would do such a thing.

God's plans and dreams for us always point to our success. No matter how much we need to learn along the way, He always desires our good. He is not only faithful, He is infinitely wise. And in a family like Joseph's (and maybe even yours) that is a very good thing indeed.

7

Two Cowards, Two Different Destinies

Most great men and women have a subtle sense early in life that they are destined for great things. This knowledge that they are the same as everyone else, yet not the same, colors their vision throughout their lives. They work harder than everyone else because they know they must rise above everyone else in order to fulfill their callings.

I believe that is true of *most* great men and women, yet sometimes greatness is thrust upon individuals who are neither ready for nor desirous of their elevation. In both scenarios—the dogged pursuit of greatness or the sheer dumb luck of it—one's character is supremely tested.

I'm not quite sure which camp I'm in, mostly because I don't believe that I have become a great man. I have made a few films that have affected millions of people, and I suppose that qualifies me to some extent, but I am also frighteningly aware of my own shortcomings and weaknesses. Most people place the sheen of a fairy tale upon greatness, and don't want to know a person's flaws if they consider that person to be wonderful. We like our heroes clean.

Yet God, through His amazing story, continues to show us that He is not in the least bit interested in presenting His characters as clean-cut, faultless men and women. I have always found it interesting how churches have a tendency to make everything look better than it really is. No divorces are happening here. No alcoholism, domestic violence or abortions. Just smiling faces and warm handshakes as you walk through the door. It is as though we think that if we can just create a sterile enough environment, then, doggone it, our environment will be clean. But, of course, God sees us for who we really are. He is privy to our angry words, gossiping tongues and secret stashes. He knows us, yet He loves us anyway.

And as we are learning, He sees things inside of us that are not yet there. He observes our wasteland and sees a tree bearing good fruit. Sometimes He has to act on our behalf to jump-start that greatness; otherwise, we will wallow in our own fear and trembling.

My own story is a testimony to this. I was a Christian who wanted little to do with Christianity; a churchgoer who hated going to church; a Jesus freak who was often embarrassed by Jesus. I wanted to live a normal life of watching movies, playing video games, hanging with friends and going on vacations. Church was an inconvenient duty. The idea of praying for others was laughable. Someone gave my wife a prophetic word during this time that one day she and I would minister to people alongside each other. It was the most ludicrous statement anyone had ever said to her. I wouldn't even pray *with* my wife, let alone alongside her for others.

Want more evidence that I was the wrong guy for this job? I rarely read the Bible, and when I did, I stuck to the Old Testament stories. That felt more like reading a book than something religious. Plus I could read about God back when He was a superhero. He'd since gotten old and seemed to have lost His touch. The God I served wasn't the exciting, devastating force of the Old Testament. He was instead a quiet, haunting presence who watched me from a distance, always with an underlying sense of dissatisfaction.

I rarely prayed, mostly because my relationship with God was so nonexistent that once I got through my litany of requests, there wasn't much more to talk about. The idea of just "hanging out with Him" was stupid. Then, when I realized that all I ever did was ask Him for stuff, I stopped praying because I felt like a jerk. *He knows what I need,* I told myself. *Best leave Him alone until I* really *need something.* But that would spin me into a downward spiral of spiritual depression, because eventually it became clear that my entire relationship with God consisted of me meekly holding out my bowl asking for more porridge. Was this it? Really? Was this all there was? I grew more and more disheartened and dispirited, and I was fast approaching the point of giving it all up. I'd still play the part, join the throngs of smiling faces and "I'm fine" replies, but inside I was ready to check out. I was becoming more interested in Christianity as art than

I was in Christ as a lifestyle. And right about then was the time God decided that I would make *Finger of God*.

So you can see why I have a soft spot for two people in the Bible in particular, because I relate to them as people who are zapped out of the blue. They are Gideon and Saul. Their stories are similar in how they began, but the character of both men took them in very different directions.

Gideon: An Unlikely Choice Makes Good

We first meet Gideon in Judges 6. The Midianites have been ravaging the land and the people of Israel for years now, and they're the biblical equivalent of school-yard bullies. Israel plants crops; the Midianites move in and destroy them. It gets so bad that the Israelites start moving their homes to clefts and caves to escape.

So Israel, as the people are wont to do, cries out to God to help them. God, of course, answers them, and we'd best pause here to examine something important. I have often heard it said that since God knows what you need, you don't have to ask Him for it. But doesn't God know that the Israelites need to be saved from these Midianite oppressors? Yet He doesn't move to defend His kids until they get to the point where they ask Him for His help. Does this mean that God is some kind of dictator who demands our attention if we are to receive His help in any given situation? Of course not.

Once again, I return to my relationship with my own children. I do not think this is an unfair comparison, because if I love my kids with my selfish, sinful heart, how much more must God love His children? God even opens up this kind of comparison in Matthew 7:9–11 when He states: "What man is there among you who, if his son asks for bread, will give him a stone? . . . How much more will your Father who is in heaven give good things to those who ask Him!"

Let's use Christmas presents as an example. Why do we have our children write out their Christmas wish lists, when we know full well what they would like (as well as what we are already planning to get for them)? Could it be that it is fun to dream with them? Is there something inherent in the human psyche that loves to be able to respond to a plea for help, or to give a good gift when asked for it?

Looking at this question from a purely practical viewpoint, the simple answer could be that no relationship is fostered when we supply our children with whatever they want even if they don't ask for it. Since God is profoundly personal and relationship oriented, it only makes sense that He desires conversation with us, even if the only time we ever talk to Him is when we ask Him for something. If that's the best we can give Him, He will take it, because any conversation is better than no conversation for God.

So here the Israelites finally call on God for help, and His eyes move across the land to find the perfect person, the perfect warrior, to lead His people to victory over the Midianites. Obviously He needs someone who is fearless, who will listen to orders without question and who will have the boldness to move forward upon God's command to do so. He needs a mighty man of valor.

Instead, God chooses a coward.

The location where God approaches Gideon could not be a less heartening sight. Gideon is threshing wheat in a winepress, which never made much difference (or sense) to me until I visited Israel myself and saw what a winepress actually was in those days. I had always pictured a spacious area like the winepress scene in the classic *I Love Lucy* episode, but what I saw in Israel was nothing remotely like that. It was more of a cleft in a rock, and it wasn't very big. A man could maybe fit in this cleft if he was small.

And this is where the God of the universe finds His mighty warrior. Gideon is hiding, doing his business undercover. He is obviously afraid of the Midianites. And this is the guy God wants to lead His army to destroy them?

Perhaps the most telling aspect of this story isn't that God approaches this guy, but rather what He says to him.

"Peace be with you, mighty man of valor."

This is one of those moments that don't make much sense in the natural, but which are actually part of God's master plan. At that moment, Gideon is anything but a mighty man of valor. But God knows Gideon better than Gideon knows himself, just as He knows all of us. He knows what Gideon is capable of; He knows the call on his life; and He knows exactly what Gideon needs to hear about himself in order that he might start to believe it.

I have already mentioned that I had a similar experience to this as I was beginning to learn about my own friendship with God. Growing up, I was always told that a relationship with God is the highest aim. But I didn't understand how I was supposed to have a relationship with someone who is invisible. I couldn't have proper conversations with Him, and, if I was honest, half the time when I was praying to Him I was wondering if I was just talking to myself.

But when I began to make my films, He began to show me more and more what a true relationship with Him looks like, mostly through the amazing men and women I was meeting around the world. Slowly, I started to grow in my understanding of Him, and I could feel myself creeping closer to a true "relationship" with Him. I knew that I had a long way to go to reach the level of the men and women I was filming: I was still too much of a screw-up, was inconsistent with my "quiet times" and generally stank at being a full-time, full-tilt Christian who pursues Him radically every second of the day. So obviously whatever friendship we had was at the stage of acquaintance. Yet my desire for true friendship with God was growing.

As I have noted, my friendship with God grew during the making of my first three films. I started *Finger of God* not even sure I believed most of what I was filming, but trying to keep an open mind. After *Furious Love*, I could feel the relationship growing; I actually wanted to spend time with the Lord and with my Bible. God began to open opportunities for me to speak in churches about this time, and allowed me to grow slowly as a "minister" of His Spirit to others. Still, I felt that I should be doing more in order to earn better standing with Him. And then I filmed *Father of Lights*, and I realized that I can do nothing to earn anything with Him. What He gives He gives freely, simply because He wants to.

The best example of my growing in understanding came midway through this journey when I was asked to speak to the leadership of a large African American church in Chicago. Up to that time, I had done a poor job of remaining consistent in my relationship with God. I remember the night before I was pegged to speak, and because life had gotten crazy, my heart sank when I realized I hadn't done my normal "spiritual prep" for this time of ministry. I felt terrible, guilty and a little frightened. My greatest fear is allowing my ministry to become a "gig," something I do on my own without my Father by my side, and here it felt as though that was exactly what I was about to do. I had fallen into that old mind-set that what I *do* affects how God sees me. I made the mistake of thinking that my faithlessness somehow affects His faithfulness.

So I drove to the church, shared my testimony and then did something I had never done. I asked everyone who wanted prayer to line up against the wall, and then I went down the line, one by one, and prayed for each person. Why? I have no idea. It just slipped out of my mouth. But, oh, I didn't just pray for them, I prophesied over all of them. I laid my hands on them, saw pictures and told them what I was seeing. As soon as I spoke, like clockwork, each person burst into tears.

When I finished, I stood there for a moment and marveled at what God had just done—what He had done through me. I had felt so unprepared, and God turned it into one of the greatest moments of ministry I had been a part of. I was mulling this over when some people approached me. They wanted to introduce me to their official prophetess, and have her pray for me. While I hadn't grown up with that particular spiritual culture, I had enough sense to know that it was a big deal.

Then the woman looked at me and said the following: "Do you know what the Lord just told me to tell you? As soon as you walked into this building, He told me to look real close at you. He said, 'You see that man there? That man . . . is My friend.'"

And as I burst into tears, I could feel my greatest religious nemesis departing from me. God did not back me up because I had earned it. He did not use me powerfully because I was such a good Christian. He did not touch all those people through me because of anything I had done. He did what He did because that's what He does. He'll use anyone, anywhere, anytime.

And then, true to form, He topped it all off by telling His kid the one thing he was dying to hear, despite the fact that I didn't deserve it in the least.

Mighty Man of Valor?

In the same way, Gideon doesn't deserve the moniker of "mighty man of valor." But, for whatever reason, this is the man God chooses for the task—perhaps because he is so unprepared outwardly. Gideon highlights his weaknesses during their first conversation.

When God tells Gideon that he's the guy who will drive out the Midianites, Gideon seems to be the only one in the room who sees reason. He tells God that his clan is the least of all the tribes, and, within this family, he's the least impressive. In essence, he tells God that He's picked the wrong person.

God remains unperturbed by this news. In fact, God replies with the only thing Gideon needs to hear—and the only thing that could guarantee victory. In Judges 6:16, God makes a simple statement: "I will be with you." These words, whenever spoken by our Father, change all the odds, rules and circumstances in our favor. It doesn't matter how impossible something seems as long as God is with us. Then, just for good measure (and because He realizes Gideon needs a major push to get over his identity issues), God touches a pile of meat and bread with His staff and sets it on fire.

That evening, God gives Gideon his first task: Destroy an idol in the village and set up a proper altar to God. This is a practice run on the way to greater accomplishments, for we are never ready for our full destiny when we first receive the call. We must grow into it, mostly for our own sake. Our character must be built up to the place God foresaw in us, and that typically comes through success with God. As God walks with us through greater and greater growth and accomplishment, we begin to see for ourselves what He has seen all along. Only then, when our character and identity have been sufficiently constructed, are we ready to step into our ultimate destiny.

Gideon is not ready for prime time yet, so God gives him a fairly small task to start with (at least in relation to what was coming next). And Gideon, the man God has chosen to lead the Israelites to victory over the vaunted Midianites, is so scared of his family and the men of the town that he does it under cover of darkness. Well, at least he does it.

The next morning, everyone is in an uproar to see that their big idol has been torn down. After a little digging, they discover that Gideon did it. They demand that he come out so they can kill him. Here's where you hope to see your hero rise and boldly proclaim that God is the one true God, and anyone who has a problem with that should step right up.

Instead, Gideon presumably hides (yet again) in his father's house and his old man is the one who has to go out and challenge the crowd to get their idol to fight its own battles.

On his first big mission, Gideon succeeds . . . sort of. But he is certainly not the man he will soon become. Something "special" has to happen first.

After this initial test, it seems as though God is happy with His pupil, and He decides to get it on in a big way with the Midianites. They've been picking on His kids long enough, and now it's time for the reckoning. We don't know how much later after the idol incident this all occurs, but at some point the Midianites make a big move across the Jordan River and are looking to bring the noise on Israel. It's now or never, it seems, and it is now when God does something peculiar. Various translations of Judges 6:34 say that He "came upon Gideon" or "clothed Himself on Gideon" or "put Gideon on like a glove." Whatever He does, His Spirit comes to rest on the chosen one, and as a result Gideon is a changed man. The one who hid in a winepress and quietly did God's bidding under cover of darkness, now blows a trumpet and calls the Israelites to arms.

What changed him? The answer is simple. The Spirit of God. God is inherently the God of the impossible, and He isn't afraid of anything. It only makes sense, then, that when our spirits are possessed by His, our minds are transformed into being more like His as well. We are able to do things we normally would never do, and we carry boldness that is often unnatural to us.

But we still retain our own faculties, faults and weaknesses. Gideon shows the blueprint of all humans who are striving to do the impossible under the influence of God's Spirit, yet still have to contend with the weakness of their own flesh. Here he basically passes the point of no return by sending heralds throughout the land to gather an army. He does this under the influence of the Holy Spirit. Immediately afterward, though, he poses a seemingly preposterous question to that same God who just caused him to start the war.

It is a familiar story to most Christians, so I won't belabor the point. Gideon lays out a fleece and asks God to confirm to him that they will indeed win this war. If yes, let the fleece be covered with dew in the morning and the ground be dry. God does it, but that's not enough for Gideon. He asks again, this time reversing his request, asking God to make the fleece dry and the ground around it wet with dew. Just in case the first miracle was, you know, a fluke or something.

There are two things that I find fascinating in this story: (1) that Gideon would even ask such a thing; and (2) that God would actually *do* it! But both actions show the character of both parties, and we do well to learn from them. We have all had our "Gideon moments," I'm sure, when we know God is asking something from us, yet we need more assurance that, you know, He *really* wants us to do this. Some people I know are stuck in a Gideon moment, perpetually waiting for one more sign from heaven that they are supposed to step out in faith and do what they think God is asking of them. I have a feeling, though, that if Gideon had kept this up much longer, either God would have stopped doing it, or Gideon would have awakened one morning to find that *he* was covered with dew!

But God again shows hints of His personality here, especially toward those He has chosen as His friends (for reasons only He can explain). He knows that Gideon doesn't feel ready for this job yet, but the time is now, so He "puts Gideon on like a glove" and enables him to jump-start his own destiny. Immediately after, Gideon's flesh seems to kick in, and he's back to being the scared, cowardly man who needs lots and lots of assurance. But God indeed does reassure him, very patiently in fact, and eventually Gideon is resolved to move forward. You get the sense in this story, more than most in the Bible, that God is dealing with immaturity and lack of faith, yet He handles it with grace, patience and love. He does so because that is His personality.

And, of course, God gets the last laugh. I've said it often: I am convinced that God has a very healthy sense of humor, and this story is one great example of it.

He Who Laughs Last

Understand the timing here. In rapid succession, Gideon receives the call (in the winepress), steps out tepidly to answer the call (his nighttime escapade), is overtaken by the Spirit of God (to do something he normally would never do) and shows his own lack of trust in God (the fleece). Sometimes our friendships with God do not have the luxury of years and years of development. Sometimes He puts us on the fast track to relationship and trust—whether by necessity (the Midianites are attacking) or simply because we are wired a certain way.

Gideon probably thinks it is enough that he agrees to lead this army against the feared Midianites. But God has bigger lessons in mind, and He is going to show Gideon once and for all, in one giant act, what can happen when you put all your trust in Him.

As they're getting ready to fight, God tells Gideon that he has too many men. I can just see Gideon's heart sinking. Seriously? You're pulling this on me now? Say what you want about God, but He doesn't always make things easy. Children who have to work for what they receive are always better off than children who are given everything without working at all.

So God goes through the now-famous weeding out of soldiers until Gideon is left with three hundred men to try and defeat an army that has so many camels they can't be counted. I'm jumping fully into conjecture here, but if we're talking about God's personality as shown through this story, it's hard not to see Him sitting back at this point, looking at three hundred vs. tens of thousands and thinking, *There we go. I like those odds.* It's as if He's purposely making things difficult either to make it more interesting to Him (He is God, and even God needs a challenge every once in a while), or because He wants to teach Gideon and the rest of humanity a lesson in trust. Maybe it was a little of both.

In exploring God's personality in friendship, I am always amazed at how much He knows us, and how He always seems to know exactly what we need at any particular moment. Whether it's an encouraging or prophetic word, "stumbling" across a verse in the Bible, or a meaningful email out of the blue, He is always faithful and always on time. Gideon's story is no different.

At this point, I have to believe that Gideon is wishing he had never signed on for this mission. This whole thing has gotten more impossible by the minute, and now God is asking him to do something completely ridiculous. How are three hundred men supposed to defeat a massive army? Yet God knows Gideon's heart as well as what he needs, and their next conversation is a telling one.

That night, God tells Gideon to go down into the enemy camp. He wants to reassure Gideon, as any good Father who has a son who needs constant reassuring would. But if you read between the lines of His statement to Gideon, you can see something of His desires for the situation, even though He seems to know what Gideon is going to choose.

> It happened on the same night that the LORD said to him, "Arise, go down against the camp, for I have delivered it into your hand. But if you are afraid to go down, go down to the camp with Purah your servant, and you shall hear what they say; and afterward your hands shall be strengthened to go down against the camp."
>
> Judges 7:9–11

God wants Gideon to go into the camp by himself. "But if you are afraid," He says, "take your servant with you." Taking his servant is God's second choice for Gideon—He makes that clear. Gideon, in turn, shows his inner turmoil when he indeed does take his servant with him. This is interesting because no matter whether Gideon goes alone or takes his servant, the same thing is going to happen: Gideon is going to overhear the Midianites admitting their fear of him. So why does God give Gideon two choices even though He obviously wishes for Gideon to go alone?

The answer, as always, comes down to friendship and relationship. God is trying to build a *personal* relationship with Gideon. He wants to be Gideon's friend, and so He suggests that just the two of them go together to experience this special moment. But Gideon can't bring himself to trust God enough and brings a "third wheel" to something God was hoping would just be for them.

When my first daughter, Serenity, was born, my mother-in-law, Carol, had to struggle with a few things. I'm sure this is fairly common, but she had a hard time coming to grips with the fact that she was now a grandmother. The idea was terrifying to her (and it also, I think, reminded her of her own mortality). We laugh about it now, but at the time, she was so scared of her reaction to seeing her first grandchild that when she came to the hospital for the first time she actually brought a friend with her! Of course, as soon as she laid eyes on Serenity her heart melted—and her friend instantly became persona non grata in that very private moment.

Years later, when we talk about this, Carol admits that her own fears and issues at the time infringed on that special moment of hers—a moment that was supposed to be just between her and her granddaughter. Some things, it seems, are meant to be shared just between two people. For Gideon, this was just such a moment, but his own fears and issues got in the way.

And of course, God proved to be utterly gracious about the whole thing, even telling him it would be okay if he brought someone else (knowing full well that as soon as He opened that door for him, Gideon was going to walk right through it). But He was gracious to Gideon because that is who He is.

Judges 7:13–15 provides the climax of this budding friendship, and it reveals God's plan all along regarding Gideon.

He goes down to the camp with his servant and overhears the soldiers admitting defeat before the battle even starts. In one fell swoop God removes all doubt, fear and stress for Gideon. He, in essence, gives Gideon exactly what he needs (and wants).

As soon as Gideon hears this, the Bible says "he worshiped God." The aim of everything that God does in our lives is ultimately to get us to this place with Him. He does all that He can, provides us with as much as we need, works behind the scenes constantly, fights invisible wars on our behalf, sacrifices His own Son and essentially obsesses about us so that we might one day see what He has done for us. And all He wants in return is for us to worship Him. To trust Him. To talk to Him. To rely on Him.

He wants us to be friends with Him.

Saul: Rejecting the Invitation

And then there's Saul.

I included Gideon and Saul together in this chapter because they have a number of similarities in their stories, yet Saul careens off in a completely different and tragic direction. This is important to note because as much as it reveals the darkness of the human heart, it also shows what can happen when friendship with God is never fully realized even after God has invited it.

We first meet Saul when he is a young, strapping man, described with these words: "There was not a more handsome person than he among the children of Israel. From his shoulders upward he was taller than any of the people" (1 Samuel 9:2). He is what you would think a king would be. In essence, he's the cool one that everyone agrees is the right man for the job.

Once again, the people of Israel are in trouble and, as a result, they cry out to God to help them. They want a king, they say, because everyone else has a king. This could be the single dumbest reason to ask for a king, but, hey, they're human. I used to look at these kinds of decisions made by the Israelites and feel good about myself, because at least I wasn't *that* pathetic. But then I realize all the idiotic things I have asked God for, and suddenly I'm not so smug.

So God tells Samuel that He'll give them what they want, much to Samuel's surprise. We are then treated to a wild goose chase as Saul goes in search of some lost donkeys, which culminates in Samuel meeting Saul and telling him that he is to be the king of Israel. That would be a fairly heady conversation for sure, and Saul's thinking on the matter is revealed pretty quickly. When the time comes for Saul to be crowned king, he is nowhere to be found.

Saul is, in fact, hiding among the baggage when time for his coronation is at hand. This is eerily similar to Gideon trying to talk God out of choosing him for such a big destiny. It reveals Saul's heart for this appointment at this stage—he doesn't feel he's ready, and he doesn't feel he's worthy. These seem to be the kinds of hearts God enjoys elevating the most, because only God would ever do such a thing. I have filmed with so many people—from drug-abusing Todd White to Indian gang leader Ravi—who on the outside were the worst possible choices by God to do great things for His Kingdom.

But if you read His book and understand the story He is telling, it becomes painfully obvious that He does not look at your pedigree; nor does He look at your qualifications. He looks at the very depths of your heart, and what He finds there determines the kind of call you will receive from Him.

Since Saul was the first man in history to be crowned king over the Israelites, it stands to reason that God saw something in this man's heart that impressed Him. Saul certainly didn't start out with a haughty attitude or an overinflated sense of himself; otherwise he wouldn't have sneaked off to hide when his big day came. Saul did not ask for this; nor did he particularly want it. At first.

At the risk of getting into some deep theological territory, I think it is time to say something about the importance of our choices. My take on this comes from what I read in the Scriptures as well as what I have seen and heard from people around the world. Could I be wrong? Of course. Feel free to examine the Scriptures yourself to come to your own conclusion. But this is what I see.

I have had the same conversation with thousands of people. And everyone believes that he or she has received a promise, a call from God. But this is the thing about promises: There is no guarantee that the promises of God will be completed in our lifetimes. The Bible is littered with promises from God that weren't fulfilled until after that person's death. Hebrews 11 lists a veritable who's who of the Bible—Abel, Enoch, Noah, Abraham, Isaac, Jacob, Joseph, Moses, Gideon, Samson, David, Samuel, the list goes on. They were all commended for their faith, but none of them received in full what had been promised (see Hebrews 11:39).

God is weaving together the largest, most intricate story that could possibly be written, and, as any writer worth his salt knows, the overall story is more important than the individual plot lines. It just so happens that our lives are themselves the plot lines of the Father, and because of His great love for us, He has given us a good deal of say in the way our plots turn out.

He's so intelligent He can work with whatever we give Him—even if we give Him nothing (He'll simply go to work on another plot line in an attempt to weave it into His overall purposes). And just in case we start to worry that God is weaving His plots from afar, never fully engaging us on an emotional level, let me remind you that He is the one author in all of history to care so much about His characters that He personally entered His story and allowed His Son to be brutally murdered on our behalf precisely so that our stories could eventually lead us straight into His heart.

The First Step

There is a difference, then, between the promises of God and the destiny of God. His promises for us are a part of the larger story He is weaving throughout history. Eventually, when it's all over, He is going to blow our minds with how He has intertwined them all together over thousands of years. But that time has not yet come, and we must simply play our part in the larger story that we don't fully understand.

The destiny of God is different. It is the call He has placed on our lives—it is His ultimate *desire* for our lives. Our destinies will always hinge on one thing, and one thing only.

Faith.

Hebrews 11, the same chapter that names people who never lived to see their promises fulfilled, also makes perfectly clear that what these people accomplished was done by faith that God is who He says He is, and that He would listen to them. Hebrews 11:2 makes this point when, regarding faith, it says that this is what these ancients were commended for.

If faith is what the ancients were commended for, then it stands to reason that faith is what you will be commended for as well. And if you want to live the life God is calling you to, then faith is going to be the key.

I mentioned that I have talked to people all over the world, and almost all of them are living in some state of frustration with their lives because they are not yet doing what they have been called to do. Why not? They don't feel ready. They don't have the money. They don't have the support of their families. They don't know what to do. They don't know how to start. They are, all of them, afraid of the unknown. They are afraid of what will happen if they step out and fail.

When I started as a filmmaker, I was convinced it was going to fail. I had no illusions that people would ever watch a film made by an amateur who had to learn how to shoot and edit while he was doing it. I figured that there might be a small subset out there who had no interest in aesthetics and simply wanted to see some cool God-stuff on a video—and those people were my only hope going into this thing.

I have since discovered that most of the people who are afraid of failing when they feel the call *never* move forward because of that fear. That is why so many people are prowling around the starting line, anxious and nervous that they're going to run badly, when all they need to do is put one foot in front of the other and step forward *in faith*.

The first move toward your destiny, therefore, is stepping out in faith. But that is only the beginning. Once you have done so—once you have taken the initiative—that's when the real test begins.

"Recalculating" After Those Wrong Turns

So what does all of this have to do with Saul? It's simple. Like so many of us, Saul does not believe that he is worthy of the call God has placed on his life; he is afraid of trying to fulfill his destiny. Further, Saul's is the best cautionary tale available of what *not* to do when you move forward in obedience and faith.

First Samuel 10 tells the story of Saul receiving his commission from Samuel to be king, and learning what is going to happen once he leaves that place. There is a curious moment when Samuel tells him:

> "The Spirit of the LORD will come upon you, and you will prophesy with them [a procession of prophets he will meet] and be turned into another man. And let it be, when these signs come to you, that you do as the occasion demands; for God is with you."
>
> 1 Samuel 10:6–7

I find two things striking here. One, it takes the Spirit of the Lord to come upon a person before he or she can be truly changed. But then again, as we shall see, while Saul was a changed man, his flesh was still very much something he was going to have to contend with. And as we shall also see, he did not contend with it well. Two, and this is perhaps one of the strangest statements of all, is Samuel's recommendation that, once the Spirit has come upon him, he should do whatever he wants to do, for God is with him.

I meet people constantly who are racked with confusion because they don't know what God wants them to do. If only they could get an email from Him, they say, telling them exactly which of the possibilities in front of them to take, then they would gladly and faithfully do whatever He says. But no email comes, and they, like so many others, continue to sit around and wait.

God is with you implies friendship. While I caution against extrapolating too much from this one verse, I think that in some circumstances, certainly, the statement applies to us. If God is your friend, if He is truly for you, then in a sense it doesn't matter what race you choose to run. God's overall destiny for you is not going to be affected by the choice you make right now.

So many of us are terrified that we're going to miss it, that we'll run the wrong race and will move further and further away from our true calling. But the reality is this: If God has indeed placed a specific calling on your life, you're not going to be able to escape it.

My friend Ravi says that God explained it to him like this, at least in regard to leadership. When God has placed a specific call of leadership on your life (and not everyone has received a call of leadership, mind you; typically you'll know deep down if you're meant to lead or create something, or if you are called to come alongside others as an armor bearer), it is as though a GPS has been attached to you. This means that if you take a wrong turn, God will simply "recalculate" and work on helping you follow the directions that will ultimately lead to your true leadership destiny in Him. So in a sense, you can't fail.

I believe this is God's message to Saul. His destiny is to be king of Israel because God has decreed it. In the meantime, Saul, do whatever you want to do, because God is with you. You'll succeed in whatever you try, because God is with you. And you won't miss the "on ramp" to your destiny because, well, God is with you. Essentially, Samuel is telling Saul that the pressure is off. God has this one covered.

It's the same thing I'd like to say to you. The pressure is off. God has this one covered. He is with you, He is for you, and He will get you where you are supposed to go, no matter what decision you make. That doesn't mean we aren't to ask Him about everything. He knows timing better than anyone, and while taking a lot of wrong turns won't keep us from our true destiny in Him, it *will* take us longer to get there!

It is interesting at this point that Saul is evasive when given the opportunity to affirm his calling. His uncle asks what he and Samuel talked about, and Saul relays only the part about the donkeys being found. He says *nothing* of the fact that he was just pegged to be king of Israel! Is this modesty or something else?

I mentioned the importance of choices before, and here, right at the beginning of Saul's destiny, he has a choice to make. Does he embrace his call, or does he shrink from it? God has just changed him, and he has just experienced the power of the Holy Spirit, yet his identity has not yet been changed. He is still fearful, still hiding among the baggage. Does not God's touch change *everything* about us?

Apparently not. God's touch, I believe, empowers us to do what God is calling us to do, and provides us with an experience to draw upon when faith is required in the future. And it certainly changes our attitudes and hearts and minds. But it does not override the flesh. That is left for us to do. If our flesh weren't present, we would have no need for faith, because we would simply *know*. Once we die and have "shuffled off this mortal coil," then we will know. But until that day, we will always have two realities to deal with. The reality of God and the reality of ourselves.

We have choices to make, especially once we have set off down the road God has marked for us. As I said before, most people I meet are standing still and are frustrated precisely because they are unwilling to make a choice. They want God to make it for them. But God wants us to be free, and freedom brings with it choices.

You are free to choose Him or reject Him. You are free to trust Him or to trust your own understanding. You are free to take a step forward or to remain where you are. It's up to you. He will love you regardless, but don't be surprised if He doesn't use you much. He can only work with those who choose to step out in faith.

Show, Don't Tell

Saul's reign as king starts off well enough, and he succeeds in uniting Israel to win his first battle, thus securing himself as king. But it doesn't take long before his own heart betrays him—and it is here that we must pause, because it reveals as much about the part we play in friendship with God as it does about God Himself.

Another big battle is about to take place, this time with the Philistines, and this is going to be Saul's first big test of faith. Just like Gideon, Saul faces soldiers "as numerous as the sand on the seashore" (1 Samuel 13:5 NIV), and just like Gideon's fellow Israelites, the people are so afraid they are fleeing to rocks and caves to hide from the invaders. Everyone around Saul is terrified, and many of his soldiers are fleeing as well.

Samuel tells Saul he'll be there in seven days, and at that point he will inquire of the Lord as to what they should do. On the seventh day, though, Saul panics because he doesn't think Samuel is coming and he's losing his troops. He decides to set up the burnt offering and do it all himself. Right after this, Samuel does show up, and, boy, is he ticked off. This is the end of Saul's reign as king. Almost as soon as it started, it's over. Samuel's ticked, God is ticked and Saul tries to explain himself.

Growing up, I always read this story with a sense of sorrow for Saul because it seemed to me that he got a raw deal. He made a bad judgment call; he panicked, and it was a one-time mistake. Why, then, is God so angry with him? And if God gets that angry over one mistake from the guy He's anointed to be king, what is He going to do to me when I continue to screw up? It's one of the reasons I tried to avoid the Father for so long. I didn't trust Him, and I was very afraid of Him.

But that was before I truly understood friendship with God. Look at Gideon's army again. God pared it down to three hundred people not because He's a narcissist who wants to look amazing, but because asking us to do the impossible is the only way He can keep us from thinking we are the ones doing this stuff. He doesn't want us to rely on ourselves because that would, in turn, lead us to ignore the relationship He so desperately wants with us.

God is asking for faith and obedience from us. Is this because He's a bully with a need to dominate? Of course not. Remember, because of His nature, He is forced to remain an invisible presence in our lives, and the thing He wants above all else is our love. My wife has told me time and again that it's not my words that show her I love her, but my actions. If I tell her I love her every morning then completely ignore her requests and desires, then I am showing her quite clearly that I don't actually love her. Words of love and praise mean little unless they are backed up by actions.

God is not a gun-toting redneck with a short fuse; He is loving and patient and kind. He gives us *everything* in love, and asks only for our love in return. But how can He know that we love Him except by the fact that we trust Him and do the things He asks of us?

Saul was given a direct order from God to wait for Samuel. Saul was king, but he was not to be a king like all the other kings. He was to be subject to God, the one true King. By ignoring this directive, Saul proved he had no faith in God. He had faith in the religious activity surrounding God (hence his desire to hurry up with the proceedings), but as he watched his soldiers running away, he no longer trusted in the word of God.

Gideon, on the other hand, had to sit and watch God systematically dismantle his army in the face of a terrifying enemy. It must have been excruciating. When he was left with three hundred men, he was still frightened (remember, he brought his servant with him down to the enemy camp), but he stood his ground and trusted God. He had faith that God would be true to His word.

Saul had no faith. And since God sees the heart of man, He knows pretty quickly that Saul is not going to be able to stand up to his own flesh. God has done everything He can to ensure Saul's success. He has changed his heart and filled him with His Spirit of power. In the end, though, the choice to have faith in God is left entirely up to Saul—and to us. That is the one thing God cannot force on us, because it is the one thing we can do to show Him our love. ·

This is not a one-time slipup, and God knows it. It doesn't take God much time to size us up, that's for sure! Later, in another battle, Saul is told to lay the place to total destruction and he disobeys once again. He allows the conquered king to live, and saves some of the best sheep they capture "to sacrifice to the LORD" (1 Samuel 15:21). This is a man who just doesn't get it, and Samuel lets him know exactly what he doesn't get when he tells him (and us): "Has the LORD as great delight in burnt offerings and sacrifices, as in *obeying the voice of the* LORD? Behold, to obey is better than sacrifice, and to heed than the fat of rams" (1 Samuel 15:22, emphasis added).

To put this in modern language, God is saying that to obey His voice is better than any alternative we might propose, even if that alternative is quite religious—like going to church and singing worship songs. Saying you love Him is one thing, but obeying Him proves it.

There is also a telling comment just before this, when Samuel and God have a conversation about Saul, and Samuel gets the bad news from the Big Man Himself. God actually tells Samuel that He is sad He ever made Saul king "for he has turned back from following Me, and has not performed My commandments" (1 Samuel 15:11).

The greatest rebellion we can commit against God is the rebellion of our hearts. To think we can do it all ourselves—to believe that His Kingdom rests on our shoulders, to elevate ourselves to His place as King in our own lives—is the fatal flaw of far too many of us. It is the primary reason He is not moving in many of our lives today. Until we submit to Him and allow Him to be our true King we will be forever frustrated, because the natural order that He desires is disrupted by our arrogance and fear and lack of faith.

If you continue to read Saul's story, you will see that God's assessment is indeed correct regarding this man's dark heart. One gets the sense that God is hoping he will make the right choices, that somewhere in his heart is the ability and desire to do what God wants him to do. Ultimately, though, power, prestige, fear of man and lack of true friendship with God lead him to his downfall.

Darkness Falls

Saul reaches the bitter depths when the Philistine army is once again on the horizon and Samuel, his trusted advisor, is dead. Saul visits a necromancer (one who talks to the dead) in order to call up Samuel for advice. His relationship with God has been destroyed, and his only hope now is to turn to the dark arts in a shortsighted effort to regain the counsel of the Father. First Samuel 28 is certainly in my top ten of strangest chapters in the Bible. Not so much because of what Saul does (which is evil), but more for the fact that it actually works!

This scene reads like something out of a Hollywood horror film. It's nighttime and Saul disguises himself (proof he knows that what he is doing is wrong), and brings two friends with him for moral support. Saul assures the medium she won't get into trouble, tells her he wants to talk to Samuel, and she does her thing. When Samuel actually appears, the lady freaks out (either because it's never actually worked before, or because she realizes somehow that this is the king in front of her). At this point, she gives Saul an out to stop this madness, but he tells her not to worry, and asks what she sees. You can just see him sitting there, leaning forward in his seat, having gone so far down this crazy trail that he no longer knows right from wrong and only cares about saving his own skin.

What is most disconcerting to me in this story is the fact that what Saul is doing is 100 percent wrong; it is witchcraft, which God detests. Yet Samuel actually appears and speaks to Saul. He seems to know what is going on, and prophesies to Saul that the next day he and his son will die. I have nowhere to put this in my theology, so I will just accept it for what it is. But the thing I most want to focus on is what Saul admits to Samuel.

Saul acknowledges that God has abandoned him and explains that he has done this thing in order to ask Samuel, who is dead, what he should do. Even at the end, Saul simply doesn't get it. He has spent his entire reign, the entire path of his destiny, either acting rashly, working to protect his own title or asking others what he should do. I have seen this time and time again as I travel to various churches and conferences all over the world. People are wondering what God wants them to do, so they jump from church to conference to event hoping that they will encounter someone who will make a decision for them. They want to hear the voice of God, but they don't trust their own ears; so they look to others.

But as much as God loves prophecy, it ceases to be edifying when it is used as a crutch. The final mistake in Saul's life reveals his true heart. He is not interested in a relationship with God. He is interested in God only so much as He can help him survive and prosper.

And, of course, God understands this, which is why He rejects Saul as king. Instead, He turns to another man, another candidate for this destiny. His eyes come to rest on a young shepherd boy. A "man after God's own heart."

8

The Murderer After God's Own Heart

When you're writing a book about what it takes to be friends with God, finding someone in the Bible who carries the moniker "a man after God's own heart" seems pretty much like a godsend. After all, isn't that what friendship is in a sense? Two people whose hearts have bonded together—where you are just as concerned about what is on that person's heart as what is on your own?

David, obviously, is a lynchpin in God's story of redemption for this planet, and I wonder if much of the reason God made that decision was the fact that, well, David was His friend. David cared about God's heart, about what God wanted, and as a result, David saw astounding success in all that he did. He was rewarded beyond measure for his faith and trust in an invisible God. For all intents and purposes, the story of David in the Bible seems like the ultimate fairy tale of friendship with God.

But then I sat down to read the entire story of David again, and I couldn't help but notice a few things. Much has been made of the fact that David was an adulterer and a murderer, and, don't worry, we'll get to that in a moment. But David poses other problems as well, which I suppose can be played off to the culture he existed in. I mean, David was one violent dude. He was covered in blood, which is one of the main reasons God didn't want him to build Him a permanent Temple, but instead passed that job off to David's son Solomon.

I don't want to horrify you too much, but again, sometimes we read these stories and gloss over them because we've heard them so many times. I assume you know what is involved in removing an uncircumcised man's foreskin. The mental picture itself is terrible enough, but now add to that the fact that David, in order to earn Saul's daughter as his bride, did that to two hundred *corpses*, and I think you start to get the idea. David may have been a man after God's own heart, but he is decidedly not a man I can relate to. I freak out when I get a sliver in my finger!

We can be thankful that God is not calling us to be like David in his actions (although, as we will see, we can learn a lot from him), but He is revealing much of Himself in how He treats and responds to David in His budding friendship with this warrior king.

Get Over It

I find something inherently comical in the way Samuel is told to find the next king (yet Saul—even though God has rejected him as king—will continue to hold the throne for more than a decade). This is another one of those stories I just glossed over growing up once I learned how the story ends, and I never really stopped to consider the particulars of God's choice of David as king. If I had, I would have wondered about a few things for sure. . . .

In 1 Samuel 16, we find Samuel mourning God's abandonment of Saul as king. Saul has revealed his heart, as we saw in the last chapter, and God simply cannot have someone with that kind of character leading His people. So God comes to Samuel and, in a somewhat cheeky tone, asks him, "How long will you mourn for Saul?" It seems an odd thing for a loving God to say—the cosmic equivalent of an impatient husband saying to his wife who just lost her cat, "How long are you going to be like this? I want to go out to eat." It doesn't seem too . . . shall we say . . . sensitive. Now I'm willing to chalk this one up to my not being present for this conversation, and I realize that the tone of this admonition might have been different from what I imagine. But whatever the tone, God's purpose is made clear to Samuel: Let's go, already. We have work to do.

I mentioned this story in my first book, *Filming God*, but I think it bears repeating here considering the nature of what we're talking about. While I was not present for this conversation between God and Samuel, I most certainly *was* present for a conversation God had with me when I was experiencing my own mini-crisis.

I had released *Finger of God* about eight months prior to this moment, and it was doing exactly what I had predicted it would *never* do: It was becoming popular. When I finished that film, I remember telling my wife, Jenell, that I didn't think anyone in his right mind would ever watch it. It was simply the weirdest thing I'd ever seen, and I was the one who made it! It didn't contain great cinematography, and I had seemingly screwed up everything technically that you can possibly screw up while I shot it and put it together. It had a low-budget sheen that I figured would turn everyone off. I was prepared for a very, very modest response, if that.

But then I showed it to people, and everything changed. There was something on this film, something about it that made it unique. I wasn't prepared to say I had a hit on my hands because, well, it still looked the way it did. But I started to wake up to the fact that, for whatever reason, God had chosen to release His presence whenever people watched this movie. I was starting to get reports of people being healed while watching it, others getting gold teeth (huh?) and atheists being saved. Word of mouth began to spread about this strange little film that carried some kind of breakthrough for the spirit realm, and pretty soon I started to sell a *lot* of DVDs.

If you're reading this book, chances are you've at least heard of *Finger of God*, which pretty much testifies to just how far-reaching this little movie has become. But as we sold more DVDs, I started to make more money, and as I made more money, I started to experience my first real psychological crisis. I didn't know how to handle the success. This was a movie I had stumbled through the dark to make. Even the editing was miraculous, as I'd just sit every day asking God what I should do and would only edit (in my living room, for goodness' sake!) what I saw in my head for that day. God had supplied the money to make it from my family and friends; God was the star; God had, in essence, made this movie for me. And here I was reaping the benefits.

The truth is, I felt guilty and unworthy. I told God often in those days that there must be a million others in the world who would have made a better film. There must be a million people who know production, who could have brought a bigger budget to the table and who were more qualified to make a movie like this. Why, then, did He choose me? Why was I picked? Even my wife was unaware of the torment inside of me—torment because I did not know how to handle success for something I felt unqualified to create.

So as the whole thing was blowing up, and I was secretly dying inside with guilt, I got a call to go be on the show *It's Supernatural!* with Sid Roth. This is a Larry King–style show that focuses on all things miraculous. So, obviously, *Finger of God* was a good fit (and the fact that Sid is in the film probably didn't hurt either).

Now how Sid records his shows is he'll do, like, nine episodes in one day. So I flew down to Charlotte to do the show, and I was there with eight other people I didn't know (except for Jason Westerfield, who is in the movie), and they didn't know me. After a long day of filming, we all had dinner together then went into a side room of the hotel to pray for one another. I was still new to a lot of this prophetic stuff, so when it was my turn to sit in the chair in the middle of the room so everyone could take turns praying for me, I was a little nervous.

The first guy up was an African pastor who had never heard of me or my movies before that day. He slapped his hand on my shoulder and began to pray. Almost immediately, he said this: "You are asking God, 'Why you?' You are saying that there must be a million people in the world who are more qualified than you, who are more talented than you, who could have done a much better job than you did with this film."

To say I was astonished would be an understatement. I wasn't closing my eyes anymore, but was staring up at this man in amazement. How did he know this? My wife didn't even know this! Then, just as quickly, he got right to the answer. "This is what the Lord has to say to you. 'I chose you because you dared to say yes to the living God. *That* is why I chose you.'"

I felt my stressed-out chest relax as soon as he said those words, and I knew my inner turmoil was finally over. I cried, of course, because when Daddy gives you an answer to the deep desires of your heart, that's typically the only appropriate response. But this African preacher wasn't finished. He had one more thing to tell me.

"And God also says this to you. 'Stop asking.'"

That was it. A casual observer might not understand what He meant by that—or, worse, he'd think that God was being rude or insensitive. I mean, why would God tell you to stop asking for anything?

But, fortunately, this was a word for me only, and I knew exactly what He meant by it. The fact that He said it in such a way endeared Him to me even more. This was God saying, in two simple words, that it was time to get over myself, over my own issues, because we still had a lot of work to do. This was my first film; *Furious Love* was just starting to take form in my mind. *Father of Lights* wasn't even on my radar. My cartoon, *Anointed Fighters*, didn't exist. *The Greatest Fight* didn't exist. There was so much yet to be done that couldn't happen while I sat wallowing in my guilty prison.

God knows His children better than we know ourselves, and He is the greatest psychologist around. So I have a feeling that when He told Samuel to get on with it—and His words carried a little edge to them—Samuel probably not only got the point, but also laughed a bit to himself because God was meeting him in a way he would most understand and appreciate.

But that is not the thing about this story that puzzled me the most. No, the thing that puzzled me the most was just *how* God went about showing Samuel who the next king was to be.

Drum Roll, Please!

The story is familiar to most Christians. God tells Samuel to go find Jesse in Bethlehem, because He's chosen one of Jesse's sons as king. Samuel goes, is introduced to the boys one by one from oldest to youngest, and each time he thinks, *This is the one,* but each time God says, *Nope, not this one.* It is only after he meets all these sons that he learns that Jesse has one more kid, the youngest, who isn't there because he's out tending the sheep. Apparently, no one thought that David could possibly be the one, so they left him out in the fields. David is brought in, and God then tells Samuel, *This is the one!*

Now, this whole episode just seems strange to me. I'm wondering if you see it as well. Why, when God tells Samuel to go to Jesse, doesn't He just tell Samuel *then* to go find David? Does this not seem like the most logical thing to do? And by doing so we could avoid a lot of confusion and hurt feelings and disappointed egos. Why go through the whole charade just to get to David?

The answer, once you really get to know God, is that there is a certain pageantry here. Anyone who has ever had a prayer answered, especially one that meant a lot, will tell you that quite often those prayers are answered in the last minute, just before the clock strikes twelve. I grew up hearing the phrase, "God may not show up when we want Him to, but He's always on time." This whole scene with David is built with an increase of tension, *dramatic* tension, no less, with the climax coming upon David's arrival.

Make no mistake about it, God *likes* drama. He's a storyteller! He enjoys watching us discover His goodness and faithfulness ourselves, and like any good storyteller, He knows that the more heightened the buildup, the more powerful the payoff when it comes. All of His works, His miracles, His dramatic answers to prayer, come because He is trying to reach us in the most effective way possible. He wants to get our attention, to show us that *He* is doing this stuff; it's not coincidence or chance. If we see Him at work, then it might draw us closer to Him. That's His endgame. Always.

First Samuel 16:13 then concludes this scene with a wonderfully descriptive statement: "And the Spirit of the LORD came upon David from that day forward."

If ever you need an image of God's desire for you, this is it. He drags Samuel to Bethlehem, goes through all these sons, confuses poor Samuel because He doesn't choose any of the boys Samuel thinks it will be, then brings David in like some kind of Third Act reveal. He's giving David a grand entrance into friendship with Him. As soon as Samuel anoints David with oil, God, who comes across here as barely able to contain Himself, jumps upon David with the full intention of staying right there with this guy for the rest of his life. He knows He is about to be united with one of the best friends He will ever have.

David and Goliath

First Samuel 17:28–30 begins to paint this picture of friendship for us, and also teaches us a valuable lesson. We are entering the story of David and Goliath, and while this is familiar to nearly everyone, there is an interesting moment that I want to look at between David and his brothers before the dramatic fight between boy and giant.

David has been sent by his father to check on his brothers, who are engaged under King Saul in a war with the Philistines, and bring them a care package from home. David shows up in the middle of a stalemate—Goliath is terrifying everyone with his boasts and threats. No one is willing to take him on. King Saul has offered a massive reward to whoever defeats this monster.

So David arrives and hears Goliath and inquires about what's going on. And this is where it gets interesting. Eliab,

David's oldest brother, overhears David asking about Goliath and does not react well. Verse 28 says Eliab burns with anger at him, and confronts his little brother with scathing words: "Why did you come down here? And with whom have you left those few sheep in the wilderness? I know your pride and the insolence of your heart, for you have come down to see the battle" (1 Samuel 17:28).

Now this seems like quite a lot of venom directed toward a little brother who was sent by their father to bring them some food. Obviously, there are some deep-seated family issues at play here. It could be that Eliab is jealous of his little brother. As the oldest, he probably thinks that he should be the one anointed by God. But David's reaction to him reveals even more of this family dynamic.

"What have I done now? Can't I even speak?" He turns to another soldier to make sure he's got all the facts straight. Eliab then fades from the story.

This reveals a few key things we would do well to remember. David is obviously used to kowtowing to his brothers. And sniping back and forth between siblings was as prevalent three thousand years ago as it is today. For whatever reason, Eliab is not a big fan of his little brother. He even makes a dig at his "uselessness" when he asks, "Who's watching those few sheep out in the desert?" He accuses David of being conceited (which is possible) and claims he has a wicked heart (which we know isn't true).

The point here is that David's brother does not see him as a mighty man of God. He sees only David's weaknesses and stature; he does not see David as God sees him. God always sees our potential, whereas we usually only see someone's past. Sometimes the toughest battles we have to fight are in our own families because they are the ones who know us best—yet at the same time, they are often the last to see who we could be. Just as often, their judgments hold us back from stepping into our true calling. It takes a strong heart to ignore the insults of a family member. David, for his part, does just that. He ignores his brother and keeps pursuing the truth. Here David shows us what can happen when we don't let the fear of man affect us.

In verse 37 David is speaking to Saul, trying to convince him that this youth can indeed take on the giant warrior, Goliath. David tells him about his adventures killing lions and bears while tending the sheep, but his conviction in the protection of God is most telling of his heart: "The LORD, who delivered me from the paw of the lion and from the paw of the bear, He will deliver me from the hand of this Philistine." There is something disarming about someone who has complete, utter confidence in God—probably because that kind of faith carries power with it. Years in the fields becoming friends with God have grown in David a healthy and strong sense of trust in his Father.

Now, 1 Samuel 17:40 always confused me. The fact that David went down to the stream and chose "five smooth stones" seems like such an odd detail to include in this story that it must carry meaning. Why five stones? If his faith was so strong, why not just choose one? Or three?

But then as I put myself in David's shoes, I realized something. For all of his confidence in God, for all of his bluster that God is going to take care of business on his behalf, David is still scared.

I have mentioned that in *Father of Lights* I went to India to film with Ravi, and the plan was pretty simple: We'd show up and do whatever God told us to do. One of those things was to visit the house of the most powerful witch doctor in Southern India. I kept asking Ravi what we were supposed to do when we got there, but he couldn't tell me much. I don't think he knew himself! So we went with a tenuous plan to "preach the Gospel" to him.

This was, beyond a doubt, the most frightening thing I've ever done in my entire life. Forget thrill rides, scary movies or my wedding day, this little adventure of ours was another level of scary. A few months earlier, this witch doctor had made national news when he went to a pastor's house and cursed him and his wife. They were both dead three days later.

Needless to say, my wife was brought into this decision. I wasn't going to go if she wasn't comfortable with it. When she sought God on it, though, she had complete peace, and even told me that God would go before us on this mission. That was enough to get me out the door, but it didn't assuage my fears.

Walking toward that witch doctor's house, I *knew* I was doing what God was calling me to do, and deep down I knew He would take care of me. But that knowledge did not remove the fear caused by stepping out in obedience. Once we arrived, as is documented in *Father of Lights*, it didn't take long to realize that not only was there nothing to fear, but that God had actually gone before us and won the battle before we even showed up! The moment I heard that the witch doctor was hiding inside his house because he was afraid of us, all my previous fear washed away instantly.

While I was facing a witch doctor, David was facing the ancient equivalent of a Navy Seal—a career warrior who was a physical specimen of the highest order. He wouldn't be human if he wasn't afraid. So he picked up five stones. He was a good shot, but he was also facing an intelligent, talented foe. It's amazing he didn't pick up twenty!

Then we come to the climactic moment. David approaches Goliath with his sling, and the taunts begin. You get the sense that Goliath is insulted by having to fight this kid, but, hey, a soldier is a soldier in his book. It's just another notch on his very large belt.

And of course, true to form, God dispatches Goliath in one shot. David could have picked up one stone after all. God's faithfulness will always outshine our faith.

The Importance of Motive

First Samuel 17:46 gives us the key to David's victory against the giant. In this verse, we read David's ultimate motive. After Goliath made his boast, David made his own: He would kill Goliath; he would cut off his head; and the whole Philistine army would be fed to the birds of the air and the beasts of the field. Why? "That all the earth may know that there is a God in Israel."

That's it. That's the key to it all. David did not do this for riches or for the hand of the king's daughter, as might be implied by his earlier questioning of the soldiers. When the battle began and all pretense was stripped away and he was left staring at an impossible outcome against an impossible enemy, the true heart of David was revealed. He was God's friend. His only desire was to make God famous.

When I started making films I had very little understanding of how God works, and especially how the world of the supernatural and operating in that world works. But I learned a few things along the way, and one of the biggest lessons was the difference between *motive* and *gifting*. I used to think that only people with the "gift" of healing or the "gift" of prophecy could do that stuff, but when I saw ordinary people doing impossible things and I saw myself doing impossible things, the truth began to dawn on me.

Sure, there are people who have been gifted in certain spiritual areas, and when they operate out of that gifting God responds in kind, because a gift from God, once it is given, is never taken back. This is not magic, as if God is a tame animal who can be brought out to do our bidding; rather, it tells us something about gifting. At this point, I cannot deny that some people have been given an abnormal ability to operate, for instance, in the prophetic or in healing. But the most potent force for change in the Kingdom does not come through those lucky ones with a gift. The most potent force for change is found in something we all possess called motive.

Our motives color our spirits, and since God knows the secrets of our hearts, He always knows our motives. When you step out to pray for someone, or try to do something that is beyond what you could normally do, there is a motive behind that action. It might be to bring freedom; it might be to stroke something in your own ego; it might be to make up for something you are lacking in your relationship with God. Who knows? It could be many things. But the motive that does the most damage against evil is and will always be the motive simply to make God famous.

Sometimes You've Got to Improvise

Something about my films, I have found, causes people to approach me and tell me their life stories or their struggles and what they are doing to cope with the problems in their lives. They see elements of great faith in what I film, and it inspires them. But sometimes I worry that it might inspire people a little *too* much, especially when common sense is forced to take a backseat to their radical thoughts.

Look at the episode of David fleeing to Gath and acting like a crazy person.

> David took these words to heart, and was very much afraid of Achish the king of Gath. So he changed his behavior before them, pretended madness in their hands, scratched on the doors of the gate, and let his saliva fall down on his beard.
>
> 1 Samuel 21:12–13

This is a great example of something that I fear too many Christians overlook when it comes to facing problems. David has just fled from Saul—whose jealous heart sends him into rages against the popular young man—and has gone to the land where his natural enemies live. Word gets back to him that the servants of the king in Gath are chirping that David can't be trusted—best to do away with him now.

So David finds himself in a bit of a pickle. He can't go back to Israel because Saul wants to kill him, and he can't stay here because the king of Gath will probably kill him, too. Among many Christians I meet, this would be the time to utter some platitude along the lines of "God will protect me in the presence of my enemies." While that is certainly true in many, many instances, it is equally true that Christians are being killed all around the world at an unprecedented rate, which suggests that if you are in the presence of enemies, God's protection might not always look the way you think it's supposed to look.

While most Christians probably don't face life-or-death decisions regarding their faith, we all encounter circumstances that test what we believe and how much we are going to trust God to take care of us.

I submit that there are few characters in the Bible God wants to help succeed more than David, yet here he finds himself caught between two enemies with no real extraction plan in sight. So the question is: Does he run, or does he sit tight and trust that God will protect him? God did, after all, promise him the kingdom, did He not? Would that not be enough for him to claim absolute faith in God's protective hand?

David is a man after God's own heart and, as His friend, shows a tendency to seek God's will throughout most of his life. After defeating Goliath and many narrow escapes from Saul, you would think he has earned the right to sit tight and let God protect him. Yet, surprisingly, David is required to resort here to his own resourcefulness. He comes up with a plan to act like a crazy man in order to trick the king of Gath into thinking that he's not a threat at all, but just a loon.

Life is a balancing act between good sense that acts and faith that waits, but most people miss this. On the one hand,

I have met far too many Christians who use the "I'm just trusting God" defense as an excuse for inaction, when the best decision at that moment would be to use their own resourcefulness to figure something out. I have made this mistake myself. I have been backed against a wall and found it easy to fall on the old line of thinking that, "Oh well, God will figure it out," and do nothing. Then I can blame God if something bad happens, and I can accept this bad event somehow as being God's will for my life.

Then, on the other hand, some Christians lose patience when they should just wait and trust. They advocate the idea that "God helps those who help themselves." That statement is actually anti-Gospel! God helps those who precisely can't help themselves. These Christians rely only on their own understanding. They act according to good sense and rational thought, but they never wait for God or trust Him to guide them.

Both are wrong. God wants healthy people who know when to get creative and fight, and also when to stay still and allow God to take care of business. How do you know what to do and when? It's simple. Ask.

We are called to stay in communion with God and to listen to His whisper. When I have sought His advice, sometimes I've heard Him say, *Do this, not that*. Other times I've heard Him say, literally, *Do whatever you want. I am with you.* It seems simple enough, but most Christians "have not because they ask not." If you're confused about what you should be doing, chances are you're just not talking to Him enough.

David provides for us a great glimpse of what a healthy relationship with God should look like.

Then they told David, saying, "Look, the Philistines are fighting against Keilah, and they are robbing the threshing floors." Therefore David inquired of the LORD, saying, "Shall I go and attack these Philistines?" And the LORD said to David, "Go and attack the Philistines, and save Keilah."

1 Samuel 23:1–2

This is the first of many times that David inquires of the Lord what he should do. David is a man after God's heart because he does not rush headlong according to his own desires (unlike his predecessor, Saul, who continuously grieved God in this regard). Nor does he sit and refuse to act when action is called for. He wants the Lord's will for his life, and he is smart enough to know that God is a lot more intelligent than he is. "To obey is better than sacrifice, and to heed than the fat of rams. For rebellion is as the sin of witchcraft, and stubbornness is as iniquity and idolatry" (1 Samuel 15:22–23).

David understands this not because he has received better teaching than Saul (Saul, after all, had Samuel as his teacher), but because he understands the heart of God through his own experiences with Him. A friend always knows what another friend wants.

Strengthening Yourself in the Lord

We come now to another point in his story when David's friendship with God is deepened through a horrific event. As is so often the case, true friendships are found and won through hardship, and there is no friend in the world more reliable than the Father. David's hardship begins when raiders have stolen everything that belongs to David and his soldiers—including their families.

> David was greatly distressed, for the people spoke of stoning him, because all the people were bitter in soul, each for his sons and daughters. But David strengthened himself in the LORD his God.
>
> 1 Samuel 30:6 ESV

Dark thoughts are probably swimming in the men's minds about what is happening to their wives and daughters at the hands of their enemies, and it is enough to drive them to the brink of madness. The situation is so bad that many of them—soldiers who have vowed to follow David in battle to the death—are now looking at him with new, murderous eyes. This is his fault. They made a mistake in obeying him. Somebody needs to pay for what just happened, and that judgment falls squarely on David.

Again, sometimes we must go *into* the Scriptures to see and feel the truth of the story. It is one thing to understand intellectually that the people were talking of stoning David, but if we stop for a minute and really understand the psychology of David at this moment, we see that his response is truly remarkable.

Think about your own life. Have you ever made a mistake that caused others to be angry with you—I mean really angry, like furious angry? Dishes may have been thrown, punches may have been thrown, and words like darts may have been launched with impunity. If so, then you know what it is to feel as though "the world is against you." It is an awful feeling, and one that brings depression and self-pity on swift wings. As much as we might be able to relate, though, I doubt many of us have had people so angry with us that they were seriously contemplating *killing* us! That's, like, a whole other level of contempt. Add to that the fact that not only is David bearing the responsibility for all his trusted men losing their families, but he has lost his wife and children too!

Most people, when trouble on this scale comes our way, do various things to cope. We might drink. We might drown ourselves in movie-thons with copious amounts of chocolate. We might get violent. Whatever it is, a typical response is to go inward and look for things to take our minds off the present situation. We don't want to think about it because it is too painful, so we find something to mask the pain or make us forget the pain entirely.

David, though, "strengthened himself in the LORD." This is a curious phrase. What does this mean, exactly? How does one go about strengthening oneself in the Lord?

If you read the Psalms, many of which were written by David during his times of great stress like this one, you begin to get a hint. I heard Bono once describe the Psalms as "the first blues." Here is a musician opening up his soul to God, revealing his fears and troubles, his hopes and desires, and, above all, being honest about his disappointments and misgivings to a God who actually cares about him.

David talks to God as a friend. He rails at Him, asks Him where He is in all this, pours out his troubles and heart to Him, and finally admits that he does indeed trust Him; that no matter what happens at least he has his God. This is friendship in its purest form.

True friends listen to us, lend a shoulder to cry on and remind us of what truly matters. When all seems lost, they simply stand with us, supporting us. They might not be able to give us the answers we need, and they might have no advice whatsoever for us, but the fact that they are there to listen and not judge us—that they choose to be present in our distress—somehow, their mere presence strengthens us. God has promised that He will never leave nor forsake us. Though everyone else might abandon us or be repelled by us, God has promised always to remain loyal, always to endure our stupidity and always to be there, right next to us, supporting and loving us.

He is, quite honestly, the only friend you will ever need.

Thanking the Right Person

We now move to the coronation of David as king. For years he has been on the run—dodging assassination attempts, sleeping in caves, acting like a madman—and finally the time has come for him to strike down his enemies once and for all and assume his place as king. He is about to walk into his true destiny.

So he fights a battle and wins. He then makes a statement that is no small one. In fact, it is the primary reason for his success both on the battlefield as well as in life:

> David came to Baal-parazim, and David defeated them there. And he said, "The LORD has burst through my enemies before me like a bursting flood."
>
> 2 Samuel 5:20 ESV

165

David has done so much, has fought so hard, has defeated and outsmarted all of his enemies, yet he understands at his very core that it was not he, but God who had made it all possible. All throughout the story leading up to this we read that "God was with David," and now it ends with David's reign as king; he comes into the full promise of God for his life. After all his trials and this winding journey to his destiny, David reaches the end with his friendship intact with the Father, and as any good and faithful son would do, he deflects all glory onto his Father. This is not lip service; this is a statement coming from the heart of a man after God's own heart.

Of course, now that he is king, a new set of trials await him as he walks forward in his destiny. These trials will come much sooner than he ever anticipated.

That's One Terrifying Box

The sixth chapter of 2 Samuel is a strange one. For the sake of time let me sum it up in a few broad strokes. David is moving his entourage to Jerusalem to set up his kingdom, and he decides to bring the Ark of the Covenant with him, which makes sense as it represents God's presence among the Israelites. While it's being carried up to Jerusalem, it nearly topples off the ox cart and a guy named Uzzah reaches out to steady it. But as soon as he touches the Ark, he drops dead.

As a result of this, David gets spooked by the Ark and puts it in the house of another guy named Obed-edom (why no one in the Old Testament ever named their kid a simple Ralph is beyond me). It sits there for three months, and Mr. Obed and his entire household find unnatural favor because of it. So David arranges to bring the Ark up to Jerusalem after all, and holds a big parade as it's being brought in. David dances before the Ark "with all his might," and his wife Michal is highly offended by her royal husband's very un-royal behavior. She tells David off when he returns, and he tells her that she's just going to have to get over it because he's not curbing his passion for God for anyone. This little outburst by Michal causes her, it is implied, to bear no children for the rest of her life (a serious setback in the ancient Middle East).

Now this story has a few weird twists and turns, and since it involves the Ark of the Covenant, on which, as is stated in verse 2, "the LORD of hosts . . . sits enthroned on the cherubim" (ESV), we should probably take a closer look at this whole ordeal as it directly involves God invading His story.

As David was initially bringing up the Ark, everyone was happy. There was a moveable praise and worship block party happening (literally, they were "making merry"), and at some point one of the oxen stumbled. Uzzah reached out to steady it with his hand (which *seems* like a forgivable offense, as he was just trying to keep the thing from shattering into a million pieces), but this action, apparently, was not forgivable. Verse 7 states: "And the anger of the LORD was kindled against Uzzah, and God struck him down there because of his error" (ESV). Dang. See, this is the kind of stuff that used to reinforce my deep-seated mistrust of the Father and picture Him as some kind of bipolar deity who could fly off the handle at any moment for even the smallest offense. It's why I held on to Jesus with all my might and tried to stay away from the Father as much as possible.

Of course, as with most things I used to think, this mind-set was rooted in a complete misunderstanding of the nature and character of God.

Verse 8 states: "David became angry because of the LORD's outbreak against Uzzah." So David got angry as a result of this, but at whom? Well, obviously at God. Apparently he was thinking the same thing I was: *What the heck, God? Doesn't this seem a little, I don't know, rash?* But immediately after, David's anger turned to fear of the Lord. Literally, verse 9 states: "David was afraid of the LORD that day." Apparently, this was a new feeling for David. He had been growing in friendship and love with God, and this event revealed a new side that, quite frankly, freaked David out. If God punished this guy for doing something as seemingly innocuous as steadying a falling Ark, what in the world might be in store for David as the leader of God's people should he screw up?

Friendship does not carry with it carte blanche familiarity. Our comparisons of human friendship in relation to God can only go so far, because human friendship denotes friendship between two equals. With God, this is decidedly not the case. Few in the Old Testament understood God's heart the way David did, but even he was struck with reverence and fear when he realized the greatness and holiness he was dealing with. God is not a human, and we treat Him as such at our own peril.

While Christ's sacrifice for us has indeed opened the way to the Father's heart, free and clear, He is still God and He is still our Father. Reverence and respect must be paid to Him.

There is a reason we don't call our earthly fathers by their first names. Similarly, a balance between familiar friendship and holy respect must be struck when dealing with the God of the universe. He may be your "Abba Father," but bear in mind, God is not your buddy. You're not going to give God a wet willy or a wedgie. He may be the gentlest Being you will ever encounter but, at the same time, He is also the most ferocious.

Yet, after the inevitable death resulting from unholy hands touching pure holiness (indeed, this was the natural outcome of such contact before Christ; we're so impure that our natural bodies cannot withstand the sheer holiness of God), God resumed His nature of blessing.

David, who was already starting to show the mind of a politician, passed the problem off to someone else. He was too scared of the Ark being near him, so he made poor Obed-edom put the thing inside his house! But, of course, wherever God is, there is blessing, and Obed immediately began to reap the benefits of having God staying in his spare bedroom. David heard of this and, naturally, told Obed to take a hike when he realized the coast was clear. This episode threw David for a loop, but it is another piece of the puzzle in his understanding the nature and character of God.

This episode shows us not only God's great desire to bless us and be near His friends, but also our desperate need for Jesus to make us eternally holy in His sight. As a result of His sacrifice, we can now not only touch the presence of God and live, but also have that very presence of God living inside of us so that we might advance our Father's Kingdom as His adored children.

In 2 Samuel 6:20, this story ends with Michal, David's wife given to him by Saul—the very wife for whom he killed two hundred Philistines and cut off their foreskins (ew!)—coming against him and rebuking his zealous behavior. She came from a royal family, and, therefore, was disgusted by David's dancing and carrying on before the Ark. This is not the way royalty is supposed to behave, she reasoned, and David was not setting a great precedent as he made his way to the throne.

Now I can attest that nothing is harder for a man than his wife coming against him and rebuking him, cutting him down, or setting him in his place. But David here shows his level of love and friendship with God. Even a wife he loves and has fought for will not stand in the way of loving and adoring his Father.

Your Dreams Are His Dreams

Second Samuel 7 deals with the great blessing and promise from God to David, but it all starts with David coming to the Lord telling Him that he wants to make Him a house worthy of the God of all things. David's heart for God is evident in this request. How often have we thought how small and insignificant our words and minor sacrifices and praises are to this God who has done so much for us? Friends of God realize that true friendship must never be a one-way street where we are the ones who simply receive from Him all the time. At some point all sincere Christians have those moments when we want to do something truly significant for Him, simply because we're sick of living a life where we're constantly asking Him for stuff. David has his moment here, and his idea is to create a home for God and the Ark of the Covenant that is truly awe inspiring.

But God turns down his request . . . in a way. It is not something God wants particularly, which is shown by the fact that He never asked for such a thing. But because this is a desire of David—of His great friend—God allows it to be built. The only problem, of course, is that David is a man of war, and God wants His house built by a man of peace and wisdom. So David will have to wait for Solomon, his son, to turn his dream into a reality.

This is similar to my own children saving up their money and buying me something that I would normally never want, but is on their hearts based on their limited understanding of what Dad likes (or often and more accurately, what they like and therefore think Dad will like, too). In reality, it's not the gift that is so meaningful but rather the spirit of love behind the gift. You get the sense that God understands this better than anyone, and when He winds up giving Solomon the architectural plans for His Temple, He makes sure it meets the extravagant standards that were originally in David's heart.

But it is also just like God to do what He does next: "The LORD tells you that He will make you a house" (2 Samuel 7:11).

David tells God about his idea to build God a house, and God gently declines. He then turns it around and, taking the desire David has for Him, instead promises David his own house. The generosity and love our Father has for us is such that even when we bring a gift to Him, He flips that gift around so that it might in some way be given back to us.

171

I used to think that God was selfish. That He only cared about Himself. But as moments like this demonstrate, He is actually the least selfish being in the universe.

The Royal Screw-Up

And now we come to it.

> "'Now therefore the sword shall never depart from your house, because you have despised me and have taken the wife of Uriah the Hittite to be your wife.' . . . By this deed you have utterly scorned the LORD."
>
> 2 Samuel 12:10, 14 ESV

For better or worse, this part of David's story, his affair with Bathsheba, alongside his showdown with Goliath is what David is most remembered for. He had outstanding faith in God, as evidenced by his destruction of a giant warrior as a teenager, yet he also had outstanding moral failure that makes most of our modern-day televangelists' falls from grace pale in comparison.

The basics of the story are simple. David is king and has everything he could ever want. One day, while chilling on his roof, he turns into Peeping Tom and spies a bombshell bathing (why she isn't bathing inside is a mystery to me). David, like so many men in power before and after him, succumbs to his own moral weakness, and invites this hottie over to the royal digs, where he then sleeps with her. Keep in mind David has his own wives and Bathsheba is married as well. That's bad enough, but of course, it gets worse.

Not only does Bathsheba become pregnant, but David wants her all to himself, so he concocts a plan of cold-blooded, premeditated murder of Bathsheba's husband, who happens to be out fighting *his* battles. Predictably, what the king wants the king gets, and Uriah, Bath's husband, is killed. David is now free and clear to enjoy the spoils of his evil deeds.

Bathsheba has a son—David's son—and right about then is when God sends Nathan, the prophet, to David. God has had enough of this, and it's time for David's reckoning. Nathan tells David a story that thinly veils what David himself has done, and it gets David's blood boiling as he sees the injustice of one man taking another man's possessions. Nathan then drops the bomb that he, David, is that man, and the gig is up. Finally, David sees the light and repents for what he's done. But judgment has already been passed, and now it's time for the sentencing.

David loses his son, the one he fathered with Bathsheba; it is a steep price to pay for his sins. In God's pronouncement of guilt upon David for his actions, He uses a few interesting phrases: *You have despised the Lord; you have utterly scorned the Lord.* God makes it clear that David's actions were not simply against another man, but against Him.

Friendship with God requires two things: (1) eyes only for Him; and (2) a heart of holiness. Up until now, David has proven time and again his adoration for and trust in God. But with Bathsheba, he breaks the bonds of holiness. He sleeps with another man's wife (which is bad) then murders her husband in cold blood (which is really bad). In most any society, this is cause for the death penalty. To do something so brash and horrific is nothing but an act that "despises" God and "utterly scorns" Him. It is an action that goes against the basic fabric of human morality, let alone the standard of holiness God calls His friends to.

If you read through the entire speech God gives David through Nathan, you can hear in Nathan's words an angry Father who has been hurt by His son. There is pain in this judgment—the pain of a friend betrayed. David is punished severely, as he should be (I can think of nothing worse than losing one of my children because of something I had done), and I suspect his deep friendship with God is the only thing at this point keeping him from death as well. But almost unbelievably, forgiveness and mercy are right on the heels of this judgment.

David has made an enormous mistake, but even our mistakes, no matter how massive, cannot separate us from the love of the Father. As soon as his son dies, David worships the Lord. A lesser man (and a lesser friend) might hold a grudge against God or, more predictably, never be able to forgive himself. Yet David cannot forego worshiping his God. Their bond of love and friendship is too strong.

Second Samuel 12:24–25 completes the circle of forgiveness, and it also reveals even more about the heart and nature of God: "Then David comforted Bathsheba his wife, and went in to her and lay with her. So she bore a son, and he called his name Solomon. Now the LORD loved him, and He sent word by the hand of Nathan the prophet."

Almost as quickly as it is possible, God raises up another son for David out of the ashes of this tragedy. Human judgment is such that we find it hard to forget the bigger mistakes of people's pasts, but God operates in a level of grace that is practically unfathomable to us.

God includes a curious notation here, when He writes that He "loved" Solomon. All is certainly forgiven, and He even goes so far as to tell David so personally through Nathan—the same man He used to bring judgment down on David. This shows that God holds no grudges against us. We may hold them against others and often even against ourselves, but those judgments are false constructs built by our own anger, guilt and inability to forgive. Once again, God proves that He is infinitely more loving, gracious, merciful and amazing than we could ever imagine.

One Crappy Father

My final observation on David deals not so much with God's character as it does with our own. Second Samuel 13 tells the story of David's children, particularly Amnon's incestuous rape of his half sister Tamar. When this horrific act committed by his son against his daughter is relayed to the king, his reaction is this: "When King David heard of all these things, he was very angry" (2 Samuel 13:21).

David may be a great warrior and friend of God, but he is a terrible father. He gets angry at his kids, but does nothing. No punishment. No discipline. No repercussions. Apparently he doesn't even talk to his son about it. As a result, hatred and revenge begin to boil inside his house as Tamar's brother, Absalom, takes it upon himself to seek justice for his sister.

Friendship with God does not rid us of our flaws. Indeed, our flaws are often what keep the world (and quite often our own children) from pursuing their own relationships with God. The "preacher's kid" syndrome has become a cliché, as time and again the children of ministers, pastors and missionaries wind up being some of the worst, most self-destructive kids in the church. God is calling His friends not just to intimacy with Him, but to intimacy and a true parent's heart to our children as well. We ignore our own flaws and families at our own risk.

Friendship with God, while one of the highest forms our relationship with God can take, does not in itself bring perfection. It merely brings friendship. And while that is a high goal indeed, it is not the end of it all. In fact, it is only the beginning.

All the Weirdos
in the Old Testament

There is no question that God tells us about some really strange events in His book. There is perhaps even less question that He tells us about some really strange *people* in His book. Quite often, it is these same strange people whom God chooses to use, commune with and forge friendships with. While I prefer the company of people who are more like me (i.e., normal), God marches to the beat of His own drum. He doesn't necessarily hang with the cool crowd.

Let's face it: There are a lot of weirdos in the Bible. This chapter looks at a handful of them and the various times God either asks them to do weird stuff or does weird stuff Himself. What do these people and the way God interacts with them have to tell us about God's character? The answer, I think, is as hopeful as it is odd.

Talking Animals (That Aren't in Narnia)

Why don't we start with, in my opinion, the strangest story in the entire Bible. A talking animal. Now, this isn't the first time an animal talks in the Bible—remember that a snake spoke to Adam and Eve back at the beginning of the story, and that's pretty weird.

But the story I'm interested in right now is the one about Balaam's donkey. Here is a quick refresher from Numbers 22. The Israelites are amassing their forces against the Moabites, and Balak, their king, is freaking out. Israel is on a rampage, and since God is with them, not much can stop them. Desperate times call for desperate measures, so Balak calls up a magician, Balaam, and offers him a hefty sum if he will go out and curse these Israelites. Balaam tells him to chill while he seeks the Lord (good move).

That night, God does indeed speak to Balaam, but He tells him he must not put a curse on those people, because they are blessed.

This little conversation reveals a number of intriguing things. First, God is speaking to someone we can presume is not an Israelite, and, therefore, not a "believer." For Christians to assume that we are the only ones who can properly hear from God would be a terrible mistake. If God wants to speak to someone, He will. Even if that someone is a flipping pagan magician.

Second, He tells Balaam not to put a curse on the Israelites, because they are blessed. And herein lies a mega-interesting tidbit. Why, I wonder, does God ask Balaam not to curse His people? He is God, isn't He? So why stoop to the level of some black-magic man to ask him not to do a little voodoo on His people? What's going on here?

The answer is obvious, yet it raises a myriad of questions. God is asking Balaam not to curse His people because the curse *will affect them*. The powers of darkness are very real, and those powers carry very real consequences when unleashed. Balaam's words, for whatever reason, carry weight in the real world, and God is speaking up for His people because He knows that if Balaam issues a curse against them, it's going to get ugly.

Never think that our words don't matter. They matter a lot in this world, and we are fools if we don't remember this. From the beginning God handed His authority over to us, hoping beyond hope that we would use it for good and not for evil. Our words have power, and what we say either builds up or tears down those around us.

Which brings me to another question: Why, then, doesn't God just cancel the curse if He loves His people so much? Can't God simply make Balaam's curse not count? Can't He just block it?

Undoubtedly He can, but He chooses not to. God does not block the words He disagrees with because to do so would cancel our free will. That is how God set this whole thing up.

When I was younger, I used to play a basketball video game on my rocking Nintendo console. Built into this game was a program that adjusted the action to keep the score close. So no matter how well I was playing, and no matter how much I was leading by, inevitably my computerized opponent would make a furious comeback and the game would be close in the end. This was intended to make the experience more enjoyable for me because, after all, aren't close games more exciting than blowouts?

But in reality, it had the opposite effect. I found it incredibly annoying, and always felt a little cheated. If I was playing well enough to blow a team out, then doggone it, I wanted to blow them out. Likewise, if I stank up the joint, I didn't want computerized aid to stage my comeback—I wanted to come back on my own. This "cheating" on the game's part was done with the best intentions, but it destroyed the free will aspect of the game, which, in turn, bummed me out.

As much as we want God to step in and manipulate our lives and decisions always to tip in our favor, to do so would likewise destroy our free will. We would feel only emptiness. Life is supposed to be lived, not programmed.

It is true, of course, that when we walk in friendship and covenant with God, He does step in occasionally because He has a plan for our lives—a plan for us to prosper. Just like any parent, He wants to see His children succeed in life, and He will do what He can for us while also keeping healthy boundaries that allow us to make our own decisions and lead our own lives. He's begging us to hand the reins over to Him willingly, to trust Him implicitly, because He knows that His ways are always the best for us. At the same time, though, He will never force those ways on us if we don't want Him to (typically because we don't trust Him, and we don't trust Him because we don't really know Him). He is the consummate gentleman.

So Balaam hears from the Lord and tells Balak the next morning that it's a "no go" for cursing today. But Balak is a man accustomed to getting what he wants, so he sends more people and more money back to Balaam to try and get him to curse the Israelites. This is when the story gets weird.

That night, God tells Balaam to go with Balak's men, but to say only what He tells him to say. So the next morning, Balaam saddles up his trusty donkey and departs with the men. Numbers 22:22 then says: "But God's anger was kindled because he went, and the angel of the LORD took his stand in the way as his adversary" (ESV). Now why would God tell Balaam to do something, then be all upset when he did it? Is God schizophrenic? Obviously not, so what's up with the waffling?

To answer this question, I think we need to take a bird's-eye view of what's really happening here. God tells Balaam to go, then gets angry when he goes, so He has the donkey talk to him, then He opens Balaam's eyes so he can see the angel standing there, and *then* God sends him off with the men again! What is going on here? If God blocks his way in anger, why, then, does He let Balaam keep going after He's spoken to him? The answer, I think, is because God always intended for Balaam to go. The question isn't why God seems to be changing His mind (which He is not); the real question is why God is angry.

When I first read that statement in Numbers 22:22, I naturally inferred that God is angry because Balaam is heading out to meet Balak. But that doesn't make any sense when you remember that God is the One who sent him, and also that God continues sending him even after the donkey incident. No, God is not angry that Balaam is going; He is angry at something else. And this is where His character comes into play.

We've already seen God stoop to man's level to intercede for the people He loves. When Balaam heads out the next day, God's anger burns not because Balaam is going to curse them, but rather because someone, anyone, would actually *want* to curse His people. God has a plan in place to turn what was meant for evil to good, as we see later in this story, but the mere thought of someone wanting to bring harm to His children fires Him up something fierce.

The next time you think God doesn't care about you for whatever reason, remember this. The mere thought of others wanting to hurt you fills Him with righteous anger. *That* is the One you have behind you, in front of you and beside you. *That* is your King. *That* is your Daddy.

So Balaam sets out, and God gets ticked at the thought of something bad happening to His kids, so He . . . puts an angel on the road to stop Balaam? Wait, I thought He wanted Balaam to go bless His people, thus turning Balak's plot against him. If so, then why block Balaam's path?

Delving deeper into human psychology, I think we can see the answer pretty easily. God's intention is always for Balaam to go to Balak (otherwise He wouldn't have said to go in the first place). But He also realizes He is dealing not just with a man, but a man with whom He has no relationship. He and Balaam are not friends; they have no trust equity between them as He has enjoyed with the likes of Abraham and Moses. So He simply wants to make sure that Balaam understands the gravity of the situation.

The penultimate scene in this episode is actually quite comical. God puts an angel in front of him, but only allows the donkey to see it. Balaam beats his donkey, who is more terrified of the angel than of Balaam's whip, and, at a certain point, God "opened the mouth of the donkey" and this furry animal turns to Balaam and actually speaks!

Something else I've always wondered is why God finds it necessary to have a donkey speak at all. Why doesn't God just let the donkey stop, and when Balaam yells at the donkey, then God can open Balaam's eyes to see the angel for himself? This is what He's planning on doing anyway, so why all the theatrics with the donkey?

If this doesn't reveal loads about God's personality, then nothing does. While I'm sure there's some perfectly legitimate prophetic reason God chooses to speak to Balaam through an "ass," I also have to believe that this whole scene shows the lighter side of God. It's funny. It plays like a joke. Just look at the conversation these two have.

DONKEY—"What have I done to you to make you beat me these three times?"

BALAAM—"You've made a fool of me! If only I had a sword in my hand, I'd kill you right now."

DONKEY—"Am I not your own donkey, which you have always ridden to this day? Have I been in the habit of doing this to you?"

BALAAM—"Well, no."

Then the Lord opens Balaam's eyes so that he sees the angel—but only after this conversation. Finally, one time in human history, the animal gets to correct the master. The fact that the donkey has the mental capacity to employ logical thought gives me newfound respect for donkeys—and gives me hope that my constant baby talk to my beloved dog, Moses, isn't falling on deaf ears. Maybe he actually does understand me when I'm calling him my "precious babykins."

The rest of the Balaam story goes as God intended. The angel tells Balaam the same thing God told him the night before (thus furthering the idea that this whole thing was an elaborate setup for God—to make sure that His intentions get through Balaam's thick head, and that there will be no misunderstanding when he finally joins Balak), then sends him on his way.

Balaam arrives at the location, goes out to pronounce a blessing over Israel not once, but *seven* times, and in the process ticks off Balak in a big way. Balak, unlike most of us today, realizes that words really do mean something in the grand scheme of things, and knows that this means the death knell for him. He sends Balaam on his way, without paying him, of course, and that's the end of it.

Now, one other possibility for this story with the donkey is that Balaam had a change of heart and was indeed planning on cursing Israel on account of Balak's offer of riches. While this certainly could be true (and would also explain God's anger and sending the angel to stop him), this is an explanation we can never really know for sure because all of this would have happened inside Balaam's head, and Scripture never mentions this. For that matter, it mentions Balaam's response to Balak multiple times: that even if the king offered him all the money in the world, he, Balaam, would be able to say only what God told him to say. Whether or not this is true, we'll never know, but for now we probably need to take Balaam at his word.

Elisha: That's My Friend You're Talking About

Enjoying all this talk of curses and the power of words? Let's take a look at one of the more difficult stories in the Bible.

> Then he [Elisha] went up from there to Bethel; and as he was going up the road, some youths came from the city and mocked him, and said to him, "Go up, you baldhead! Go up, you baldhead!" So he turned around and looked at them, and pronounced a curse on them in the name of the LORD. And two female bears came out of the woods and mauled forty-two of the youths.
>
> 2 Kings 2:23–24

Oh Elisha, what a sticky mess you have made with this one. How are we supposed to extol a beautiful, wonderful, loving, compassionate God when there are stories like this one in the Bible—stories that, by all appearances, make God look like a cosmic thug on a chain of the almighty prophet? I have to admit, the first time I encountered this story in the Bible my first thought was: *Dang! Seems a bit excessive.*

As is usually the case, my first impression proved to be wrong. Yes, Elisha is excessive here, and, yes, God for some reason grants his request, and, yes, the punishment is indeed severe to the point of barbarity. How, then, does this jibe with the God of love and compassion?

Well, I think the first order of business is to clarify a few things. God is a God of love and compassion, but that's not *all* that He is. It is becoming more frequently in vogue among Christians to render God as a meek little lamb who tenderly licks our wounds as we cuddle with Him. The reality of His character, though, as is revealed in His story about Himself,

185

is that He is a warrior. He's a Lion. He's terrifying. In the midst of this, He is loving, kind, gracious, gentle, humble, etc. But you're in for a big shock if you think the God of the Bible is a pansy.

These youths (we don't know how old they are, but I'm willing to bet they're in their teens; this just seems *so much* like something an idiot teenager would do) come out and start bad-mouthing Elisha. Now, if the bears mauled 42 of them, we can probably assume that there were a lot more who got away, which makes this a pretty sizable gang. I think we can also assume that this wasn't the first time they tried to intimidate someone. This kind of behavior doesn't just happen overnight. These kids sound like your classic neighborhood punks—terrorizing those around them, causing mischief and striking fear in those who have the misfortune to pass by them. I don't for a second believe that this is a bunch of eight-year-olds.

Okay, so maybe we're in agreement that these kids are punks who deserve a good spanking. But a good spanking and a freaking bear mauling are two different things entirely. I'm still left with the nagging question of why God allowed this.

Let's start with the obvious: What were they saying? When I first read this, I thought their great sin was making fun of Elisha's bald head. My dad is bald, and we make fun of it all the time. I don't think he's ever gotten so mad at my sister and me that he wanted to send a bear to attack us. Half the time he's the one making the joke! No, upon further reflection, it becomes clear that aside from making fun of God's elect, they were taking it a step further by making fun of God. It's not the "bald head" comment that we should focus on, but instead the "Go up" one.

What happened just before this incident? Elijah was taken up to heaven in a fiery chariot that only Elisha had been witness to. Elijah's disciples didn't believe Elisha's version, and searched the mountains for the great prophet to no avail. Then Elisha was accosted by this youth gang that mocked him to "Go up," too, as if this was the dumbest thing ever to believe.

For Elisha to see Elijah's departure from the world was a holy gift, and it ensured Elisha's double blessing from God. For these kids to be going after the Almighty God like this was simply too much. They crossed the line, much as Goliath crossed the line when he hurled insults at the God of the Israelites. This, I think, was what made Elisha so angry.

So he turned and pronounced a curse. And that curse unleashed two bears on these morons. If you recall what we've just looked at concerning Balaam and his curse woes, you may be connecting the dots before I get to them. Yes, just as we saw with Balaam, our words mean something in the heavenly realm, especially if we are friends with God.

I recall how my friend Philip Mantofa, an Indonesian pastor with a congregation of more than forty thousand people, once drove past a notoriously evil nightclub in Taiwan, and righteous anger at its existence rose up in him. As he passed it he announced: "You will be gone by tomorrow morning!" A day or so later, when he picked up the newspaper, he was astonished to read that the nightclub had burned to the ground that very night.

Or my friend Ravi. While preaching in a remote village in India, he had to endure scathing reproaches from some jerk who kept yelling at him and attacking everything he said about the God of the Bible. Finally, Ravi blurted, "May you be blinded for your words!" Instantly, the man screamed. He'd just gone stone-blind. The man became a Christian shortly after (how could you not?). Ravi has repeatedly prayed for the man's sight to return, but it never has. Ravi suspects it never will.

Neither of these two men heard the voice of God or even felt the urging of the Holy Spirit to tell them to say what they did, but still their words carried weight because they are sons of the King. They are God's friends, and God listens to His friends. For whatever reason, God has granted us extraordinary power to curse or to bless those around us. He backs us up, even when we act like idiots. We're still His kids, after all, even if we do the dumbest things in the world. Say what you want about a guy going blind, but it did lead the man to salvation. Better to get to heaven with no eyes than go to hell with both, right?

Not Your Average Defibrillator

There I was, sitting in my studio one day, when the phone rang. I've since learned not to answer it myself, but for some reason I picked up the phone this time. The man on the other end was, shall we say, aggressive.

"Yeah, who's this?"

"Uh, this is Darren Wilson."

"Are you the guy who made this movie *The Fingers of God*?"

"If you mean *Finger of God*, yes."

With each sentence, I could sense his blood pressure rising. "I heard you have stuff in that movie telling people that people are being raised from the dead. You don't really believe that, do you?"

"Well . . . I filmed it, so, yes, I suppose I do."

This conversation continued on for about ten more minutes, with this man getting more and more agitated, finally ending with him accusing me of deceiving people to try and make a buck. I offered to buy him a plane ticket to Africa so he could meet these people who have been raised from the dead himself, and he summarily hung up on me.

For a better time, I should have simply sent him to this passage:

> Then Elisha died, and they buried him. And the raiding bands from Moab invaded the land in the spring of the year. So it was, as they were burying a man, that suddenly they spied a band of raiders; and they put the man in the tomb of Elisha; and when the man was let down and touched the bones of Elisha, he revived and stood on his feet.
>
> 2 Kings 13:20–21

Not much is crazier than someone being resurrected from the dead, but someone being raised from the dead by simply touching another dead person's bones? Now *that's* crazy.

You don't need a lot of backstory to understand this one. It is what it is, even if it's one of the stranger stories in the Bible. The only real question at play here is simply, Why?

To understand this story, I think we need to remember two other stories, both from the New Testament, before we can draw our conclusions. Here they are:

Now God worked unusual miracles by the hands of Paul, so that even handkerchiefs or aprons were brought from his body to the sick, and the diseases left them and the evil spirits went out of them.

Acts 19:11–12

They brought the sick out into the streets and laid them on beds and couches, that at least the shadow of Peter passing by might fall on some of them . . . and they were all healed.

Acts 5:15–16

Okay, so we've got some bones, a handkerchief and a man's shadow all performing miracles. What in the world is going on here? Are those hucksters on TV who sell the magic water and miracle hankies actually legit? (The answer to that question is a resounding no, by the way.) We have determined that God isn't some magician, yet this stuff sounds strangely like magic, doesn't it?

These three men, Elisha, Paul and Peter, were all, clearly, God's friends. They carried an anointing rarely given to humans, and were given access into the very heart of God. So, on the one hand, there should be no surprise that they did amazing things for God while they roamed the earth. On the other hand, these three stories are profoundly weird and extraordinary, and since the power of God is on full display in each of them, it must tell us something of the Giver of that power, right?

When looking at these three incidents, look at the common denominator: (1) the man being used wasn't "in charge" of the power flowing through him; and, (2) each man had been touched by God in a powerful, unique way. The first point, in

190

my opinion, is perhaps less important simply because, as we see throughout the Bible, there are many instances where a miracle is performed by someone who is fully aware of what he is doing/asking/saying. It is the second point, that these men were powerfully touched by God, that I think bears examining.

Let me give you a small example from my own life. (And please note: I am in no way comparing myself to Elisha, Paul and Peter. But the same God who lived in them lives in me, and He lives inside of you, too.) In my first book, *Filming God*, I detailed my encounter with an angel named Breakthrough, and how he pushed me to begin making my first film. As a result of that encounter, I have learned that I now carry (as do my films) a kind of "anointing for breakthrough"—indeed it is my main point of ministry when I go speak and minister in churches. This is nothing that I asked for. It was a gift given to me to accomplish what God was asking of me.

Occasionally, my wife and I feel compelled to minister together to friends or people in our community who specifically need breakthrough in their lives. Recently, some friends of ours asked us to have dinner with them. We didn't know them well at the time, but knew that we wanted to get to know them better. So we accepted and met them for a wonderful time of hearing each other's stories and becoming friends. Obviously, they heard my breakthrough story, and they made a comment that before the night was over they wanted us to pray for breakthrough for them in a number of areas. We agreed to do so, but the evening got later and later. When it was time to go, we forgot to have a formal time of prayer for this couple.

A week later I saw them in church, and they both approached me exclaiming excitedly that ever since our dinner together, they had been seeing breakthrough in their marriage and in his business that, literally, they had been praying about for years. They were receiving the fruit from a prayer that my wife and I never prayed! Now I may not have given them some bones or a handkerchief or my shadow, but I did share a nice crème brûlée.

The point, I hope, is obvious. It is not that Elisha's bones had a little bit of magic left in them, or that Paul's handkerchief carried just the right amount of anointed sweat, or that Peter's shadow transformed into "Jesus juice." Rather, the men themselves had been touched by a God who transcends space, time and even logic.

This is just as true for His friends today. When we have been touched by our Father, when our very essence has been transformed into something else, when we have been reborn as a new creation, that creation carries something that cannot be explained. It carries the power of the living God within its very bones. It carries the love of God in its very sweat. Its shadow is a deep reflection of God's goodness. Its presence can change an atmosphere, and indeed, a life.

Hopefully, the crème brûlée is good, too.

Ezekiel and Isaiah: "You Want Me to Do What?"

Poor Ezekiel. Man, does this guy get the ultimate shaft or what? There's a bunch of prophets in the Old Testament, and while many of them are asked to do some strange stuff (marry a prostitute?), no one is asked to do more oddball things than Ezekiel. Even before this strange little directive from God we're about to discuss, he was asked to eat a scroll that the Lord gave him (Ezekiel 3:1–2). What's up with this poor guy?

> "Also take for yourself wheat, barley, beans, lentils, millet, and spelt; put them into one vessel, and make bread of them for yourself. During the number of days that you lie on your side, three hundred and ninety days, you shall eat it . . . and bake it using fuel of human waste in their sight."
>
> Ezekiel 4:9, 12

Well, I suppose we'd better start with what we have. A little earlier in chapter 4, God asked Ezekiel to do a little prophetic performance art. He had to make a clay model of Jerusalem, then, like one of my kids in a sandbox, build up a mound around it to "lay siege" against it. Then, while doing this, he had to lie on his left side for 390 days (are you kidding me?), and when that was over, he had to flip over onto his right side for *another* forty days!

God is very exact in what He wants Ezekiel to do and how He wants him to do it, even telling him how much food and water to consume each day. But the kicker is when God tells him to use his own human excrement for fuel to cook his meals. Even for Ezekiel, this is too much. He complains, and God relents and lets him use cow dung for fuel instead (not the greatest trade-off, but, hey, a *slight* step up).

All this, apparently, is one giant prophetic act, dripping with symbolism, meaning and purpose, as God is placing a lot of weight on what Ezekiel is doing here. Read any commentary and it'll pretty much explain the symbolism. My question is much, much simpler than that. I think I speak for the great majority of Christians who love God and think He's awesome when I say, "What the heck are You doing here? Was there seriously no other way You could get Your point across?"

I have to admit, if God ever asked me to do something this crazy, I'd probably first try to attribute it to that burrito I had Friday night. If He persisted, I'd try everything I could to make myself think these were just my own strange thoughts. If He made it perfectly clear that this was what He wanted me to do, I'd probably bow out. Man, this one takes some serious commitment. Not sure I'm ready for that kind of dedication. . . .

But then I realize, of course, that God would never ask me to do something like this because He's my friend and He knows me better than I know myself. He knows my breaking point, and this would definitely be at the outer limits. But apparently it wasn't for Ezekiel. What kind of a relationship must you have to be able to say yes to something like *that*?

But we also have to examine why God would even ask such a thing. Why not just have Ezekiel make a general pronouncement? Write a book? Preach the same sermon for thirty days in a row? Come on, I can think of about a million alternatives to lying on your side for the length of a coming siege. But for whatever reason, God wants there to be a performance of sorts accompanying this one.

We have already looked at how important our words are, so perhaps this is an illustration to all of us about how important our actions are as well. I have often seen friends and family "fasting" from things other than food, for instance. They do this because the action of abstaining from something you really enjoy has an effect on you. Apparently, the drastic nature of what Ezekiel is being asked to do relays the drastic nature of what is coming to the Israelites. Remember, these are God's chosen ones, His beloved children, and He is obviously pained by the onslaught that is heading their way. If He didn't care, He wouldn't go to such lengths to warn them.

God has other important messages during this time to relay to His people, and He can trust this friend to deliver them. He asks Ezekiel to shave his hair and beard and burn some of it, cut some of it and throw some of it into the wind (Ezekiel 5:1–2). He asks him to dig through the city walls with his bare hands (12:7). Hardest of all, God asks Ezekiel not to mourn the death of his wife as a symbolic act to Israel (24:16)!

But Ezekiel is not the only one in God's story who is asked to do strange, embarrassing things that give a message through symbolism. Perhaps the biggest indignation in the Old Testament falls on poor Isaiah, who is asked to walk around stark naked for three years while he preaches.

> At the same time the LORD spoke by Isaiah the son of Amoz, saying, "Go, and remove the sackcloth from your body, and take your sandals off your feet." And he did so, walking naked and barefoot. Then the LORD said, "Just as My servant Isaiah has walked naked and barefoot three years for a sign and a wonder against Egypt and Ethiopia, so shall the king of Assyria lead away the Egyptians . . . to the shame of Egypt."
>
> Isaiah 20:2–4

I'll hand this to God, He sure doesn't seem to care about how He's perceived by people. In an era where we worry so much about whether or not our church services are appealing or if we're doing evangelism "right," God has His Old Testament prophets do things that would land anyone in our society in an insane asylum. Since I have no idea what the culture was like back in Ezekiel's and Isaiah's lifetimes, I can't speak to whether or not this kind of behavior designated them for the loony bin. But I'm willing to bet that it was at least viewed as peculiar by more than a few people.

Living on the Fringe

Others were asked to do strange things in the Bible, obviously, and the point here is not to do an exhaustive study of each and every instance, but rather to try to figure out what God is up to in His story by including these kinds of things within it.

I'll be honest. Growing up I heard mention of a few of these guys and what they had to do, but it was always with a smile and a wink, a kind of knowing nod to the fact that the Bible isn't *that* boring if it has this kind of weird stuff in it. But I never thought much about it, and I certainly never heard a sermon preached on it. So these men were always on the outer fringes of my faith. It was only recently, when I started meeting a few of the more radical people alive today, that I started thinking anew about these Old Testament weirdos. Returning to my original thesis that if God chose to include these kinds of things in His story, then they must serve some purpose, I found myself wondering what exactly that purpose might be.

I am convinced that if I met any of these Old Testament prophets (and I'll even throw in John the Baptist for good measure), I'd be terrified of them. I'd pass them on the other side of the street, glancing nervously in their direction, or would make a new route to avoid them entirely. They were radical to the point of recklessness, and part of me wonders if some of them might have been slightly off-kilter, if you get my drift. No matter how you look at it, these guys were strange, odd, unpredictable and more than a little frightening. Why, then, would God use people like this for such important tasks?

I think God might be trying to show us that He will use anyone to accomplish His tasks (remember His invisibility cloak problem?), and most of the time He is forced to use people many of us would consider to be "on the fringe." As I already mentioned, if God were to ask me to lie on my side for a year, I'd politely ignore Him. I'm too sophisticated for something like that. Miss an entire year of football? Gosh, that's asking too much.

But these stories are as much an indictment of the rest of us as they are testaments to His great love for us. We consider someone walking down the street mumbling to himself as crazy. God sees His kid, even someone He can use to bring love to one of His other kids. Our sophistication often keeps us from stepping out into what God is prompting us to do.

He's not going to ask you to strip naked and walk through the grocery store shouting Bible verses at the top of your lungs, but He might ask you to pray for that person standing in front of you in line. He might ask you to step out in a career that has no safety net. He might ask you to forgive the one person you promised yourself you never would.

God has big plans for His kids—for you in particular—yet there are certain steps that must be taken to get to wherever He is calling you. If you ignore or refuse His requests enough, eventually He is going to move on to someone else who is, well, more like a child.

Even as a kid, I couldn't wait to grow up. I could eat dessert whenever I wanted, could watch TV whenever I wanted and be completely in charge of myself. But now that I am a grown-up, I'm beginning to learn that growing up in God's Kingdom is actually the whole aging process in reverse. When Jesus says, "Become like a child," it is not something that happens in an instant. It's a process. When we are born, we must begin growing up. When we are born again, we must begin growing down.

These people in the Bible did what they did because God asked them to do it. He had His reasons for asking such things of them, and it is the height of our own arrogance to question Him on something we obviously know nothing about (see Romans 9:20). That they were radically devoted to God enough to do what He was asking of them is as much a testimony to their love of God as it is an indictment of our own fears.

God obviously has any number of reasons why He does what He does, but I think one of them, at least for these stories, is to show us that in the end, it really is all about Him. If He can use that crazy person, He can most certainly use you! If you've got it all put together, then typically you have more to lose, which means you are that much less likely to take a risk for God.

If you want to see and do great things for the Kingdom, then two things are certain: (1) You're going to have to face a few fears; and (2) you're going to have to get a little nuts.

10

The God-Man

U p until now, this book has focused on stories and characters of the Old Testament. I have attempted to give a better understanding of the character and mentality of God through His interactions with the various lowlifes, swindlers, cowards and murderers that make up so much of His story in the first half of His book. We should never forget that these were people of a different era, not just different cultures. I can hardly comprehend the kind of warrior and barbaric mentality these cultures embraced; nor can I understand their various customs, tribal feuds, idol worship or political and religious issues. I can only understand the stories as stories, and as such, I can only understand aspects of God's character as filtered through those stories.

By the time the New Testament begins, four hundred years of silence have elapsed between God and man, which in and of itself seems highly odd considering how personal God has proven Himself to be. What is going on in the mind of God during these centuries of silence? Is He still forging friendships with people around the world on the down low? Certainly His love for His people has not diminished. But, for whatever reason, we don't hear much. It's as if we are in the intermission, milling around the lobby, waiting for the second half to begin. And when it finally does begin—oh boy! Are we in for one doozy of a final act!

This entire book is predicated on the fact that we understand something of God's character and personality by how He reacts to people and situations. But now, with the appearance of Jesus on the scene, things get very interesting. Now instead of a God covered in an invisibility cloak, we have the very God of the universe coming to earth to take up residence as a man, just like us. We get our clearest view of His personality and friendships because, well, He's here!

What I find in Jesus not only lines up with the God we have been looking at in the Old Testament, but also shows Someone who is far better and far more complex than we usually give Him credit for. And lest we have any confusion that Jesus is somehow different from the Father, we must always remember Jesus' own words in John 14:9: "He who has seen Me has seen the Father." Whatever we find in Jesus, we can safely assume we will also find in the Father.

Of course, if we're going to talk about Jesus at all, then we had best start at the beginning.

Born in a Bunch of Crap

The birth of Jesus is remarkable in many ways, yet I, like so many others before me, have allowed it to become lost in a sea of Christmas presents, snowflakes, pine needles and fat elves. While Christmas is certainly a party, it's only vaguely a birthday party anymore. And even then we tend to do the "Jesus stuff" halfheartedly, only because we're supposed to. Sing a few songs, maybe read the Bethlehem story, make our kids remember the real "reason for the season" and that's about it. Once we feel better about ourselves, we can rip into the food and the presents and get on with what everyone really wants to do.

I don't say all this to make anyone feel guilty. I mention it only to show us (myself included) how little we think about the birth of Jesus anymore. Part of it may be the sheer repetitiveness of the imagery: a handful of people in pseudo-Middle Eastern clothing sitting around a little wooden trough with a baby (sometimes living, sometimes a doll) lying inside, surrounded by donkeys and a smattering of straw on the floor. There is usually a star hanging somewhere, and off to the side are three "Wise Men" with gifts. We have pictures of this scene in our houses. We send cards with this scene on it. We go to church services where this scene is reenacted. We watch movies where it is highlighted. Year after year, without fail, this same scene is replayed, and it's supposed to remind us of what Christmas is all about.

Unfortunately, it desensitizes us to the mind-boggling reality of what is going on—the decision by God for His Son to come to earth and share in His creation with us and ultimately redeem us.

Let's just pull back the curtain a bit, erase the Christmassy veneer and see what God is doing here. For whatever reason, God has decided that the time has come to send His Son, fully God, to this dusty, dirty world to become fully man and make the ultimate sacrifice for us so that God can get His kids back. He could do this in any number of ways—not least of which would be simply to place an adult Jesus on earth the same way He did Adam, having Him appear fully formed and ready to roll. (He is, after all, the "last Adam.") Jesus needed to be perfect and without sin when He showed up, and it seems like the simplest way to do things—have some stranger walk onto the scene from the wilderness, a holy John Wayne coming into town to clean up our mess. Yet, of course, that isn't at all what God decided to do.

Instead, God decided to impregnate a teenage girl. Himself. Is this strange to anyone else but me? Over the years we've kind of glossed over this act, but God pulls no punches when He tells us how the whole thing went down.

> And Mary said to the angel, "How will this be, since I am a virgin?" And the angel answered her, "The Holy Spirit will come upon you, and the power of the Most High will over-shadow you; therefore the child to be born will be called holy—the Son of God."
>
> Luke 1:34–35 ESV

God did not simply wave His arm or speak, "Woman, thou art pregnant," when it was time. Instead He chose to "overshadow" her. While this certainly does not imply any kind of sexual act, it does imply something intensely personal. It is part of the reason the angel, upon first meeting

Mary, greeted her as "highly favored." God only favors those He desires relationship and friendship with, and Mary was granted a kind of favor that literally no other human being has ever experienced, or ever will. All of God's actions carry the fragrance of the personal.

But there is much more to the story than the fact that God chose to usher His Son into the world through a woman. The fact that He chose this woman under these circumstances in this part of the world at this time in history is, of course, hugely telling.

Jesus was not to have the conveniences of modern-day technology at His disposal to "get the word out." In fact, He was going to have about fifty square miles to work in, and *most* of His ministry would happen along a few square miles of coastline on a little lake. The fact that in just three years and under these very limiting circumstances Jesus changed the course of world history is utterly astounding.

So Jesus (who, never forget, is God incarnate) gestates in the womb of a teenager for nine months. He is born not under the bright lights and clean sheets of a modern hospital, but instead, we can assume, by moonlight in a dirty, smelly barn. There are animals all around Him leaving excrement, and it's probably freezing.

It's as if God is telling us, right from the start, that He is not only a God who will surprise you, but He is a God who has come to serve His children in an effort to win their hearts. He is not a God of pompous vanity, but is instead One who requires nothing more than a roof over His newborn Son's head. He is royalty who carries no airs. He has never required anything more from us than our love.

God's Sign in the Yard

Have you ever seen those obnoxious giant wooden storks people put in their yards when they want to announce that they just had a baby? They do it because they're so happy, of course, and by doing so the whole neighborhood can share in the knowledge of their happiness. Hardly anyone pays attention to these things because, come on, who actually knows their neighbors these days? But at least the parents can be happy that others see their announcement.

God, apparently, was one super proud Papa upon the birth of His Son, too. And because He's God, He does the ultimate and actually writes His birth announcement in the stars! Proof, once again, that God is extravagant in His very nature.

In grade school, I was one of the Wise Men in a school play. I think I was the frankincense guy. I remember having no clue what frankincense was, but at least I was able to pronounce it right when I hit my cue. Since everyone told me that these were Wise Men, I figured for the longest time that three really smart guys showed up with presents for Jesus because they saw a big star over His barn. But then as I grew older and started understanding things better, I was appalled to learn that these guys weren't from MIT. They were astrologers! Wonder why they never told me that in Sunday school?

So we have three guys living in some faraway land who are astrologers and/or magicians (either way, they are dabbling in the occult). And while they're looking up in the heavens trying to figure out what to write in this month's horoscope, they see a message up there that a King of kings is going to be born in Bethlehem. So they set off to bring gifts to this

King, since, if it's written in the stars, it must be kind of a big deal. They look up and see God's big obnoxious stork in the sky. I think that's pretty awesome.

As much as I'd love to do a blow-by-blow rundown of Jesus' life and actions, for the sake of time and space I'll just focus instead on five stories that I find most interesting about Jesus' life and behavior while He was here, especially what it reveals about His relationship to us. These are all stories that I took for granted growing up. I never really grasped the significance of what Jesus was revealing about Himself and the Father.

Jesus Is Not a Fan of Religious People

Anyone who has read the Gospels knows that they're full of moments where Jesus absolutely lays into people, calling them names like *brood of vipers* or *whitewashed tombs*. This, predictably, offends the ones He is laying into, and it's a big part of the reason they set out to try and kill Him.

We also know the main object of Jesus' scorn: the Pharisees. Here are some of His words to them:

> "Woe to you, scribes and Pharisees, hypocrites! For you are like graves which are not seen, and the men who walk over them are not aware of them." Then one of the lawyers answered and said to Him, "Teacher, by saying these things You reproach us also." And He said, "Woe to you also, lawyers! For you load men with burdens hard to bear, and you yourselves do not touch the burdens with one of your fingers."
>
> Luke 11:44–46

The Pharisees are like the Nazis of the Gospels—the token bad guys. Whenever they show up, you just know something bad is going to happen to Jesus. Anytime I heard the word *Pharisee* growing up, I was immediately hit with a negative feeling. These were the ones who hated and killed Jesus, so they were obviously my least favorite people in the Bible. Get a little deeper into this, and you know that the Pharisees were the religious people of that day. Jesus, when He goes off on the Pharisees, is actually railing against religious people.

The word *Pharisee* carries the connotation of bloodthirsty, power hungry, fringe religious maniacs. We can pick them out pretty easily today, but that is not at all how they were perceived back then. The Pharisees were the Christian leaders, the guys with the Christian radio programs, the TV shows, the guys (gulp) making Christian movies. There wasn't a whiff that what they were doing was wrong until Jesus showed up, which was why everyone around Him was so stunned by His statements against the Pharisees, and why the Pharisees themselves were so ticked off by Him.

Yet before we get ahead of ourselves and start spouting off nonsense that God doesn't like people who are religious, we should probably define a few terms. What exactly do we mean by *religious*? Certainly we're not talking about anyone who does any kind of religious activity. Jesus makes it clear that it is not the religious person who drives Him crazy (Nicodemus and Joseph of Arimathea get quite good treatment even though they were both members of the "religious establishment" at that time).

What really gets Jesus upset is the religious person who loves his religiosity more than God and others. Essentially, Jesus gets ticked off by people who like to play church because it makes them feel good about themselves or because they find some honor in being part of a special club. Jesus came to love, plain and simple, and if you're doing anything other than that in the name of God, then He's going to have a bone to pick with you.

At this point, I've heard my fair share of horror stories from people who have been treated horribly by other Christians "in the name of love." I have talked to people who feel like second-class citizens at their churches because they don't toe the company line or attend all the events. I've heard of pastors manipulating their congregations, of people getting shunned by other Christians because they made some mistakes—I'm sure we could all pile on our own stories of Christians generally being royal-class jerks to other people. But the point here isn't to fuel the fire that all Christians are hypocrites (which we are, incidentally, and which is all the more reason we need Jesus!), but to show that there are just as many Pharisees today as there were in Jesus' time. We may not call them Pharisees anymore, but the spirit that was behind the Pharisees is alive and well in the Church today. It is the religious spirit, and it's nasty.

The religious spirit takes on many forms and faces, but generally it involves our caring more about rules, regulations, dogmas, perceptions, religious activities and behavior than we do about people. The Pharisees made Jesus mad not just because they were missing the point, but because they were actually damaging people to the end that they were being driven away from having a relationship with God.

This is the ultimate no-no with God, because, as we've seen, His main obsession is doing everything He can to have a relationship with you. When something comes in the way of His ability to do that, you'd better watch out. Jesus doesn't *care* that He's offending these people; they are coming between His children and Him—and, as such, they are going to get demolished.

It's the same as if someone came into my house claiming to be a "holy man" and tried to sweet-talk my kids into leaving with him. I don't care where you pastor or how many "apostles" you have before your name, I will not allow you to talk my kids into going with you. If I offend you and your title, I could not care less; I just want you to leave my children alone. The Pharisees were offended by Jesus because their entire identities were wrapped up in their religious activity and status. He tore into that facade and, as a result, tore apart their identity, which in turn prompted them to want to get rid of Him before they completely lost their place in the pecking order.

It might be a good idea to check your own heart once in a while to see where your true identity lies. Does your sense of self-worth come from what you do, how you worship, how you minister, or how you perform your job? Our worth rests on being children of God, plain and simple. Anything beyond that is just holding hands with the nice Pharisee man as he leads you out of your home and away from your loving Father.

Bad People in Trees

One of the great tragedies I see today, and, in fact, have seen my whole life, is the notion that people must first "clean themselves up" before they can enter a church or talk to God. This notion comes from an unwritten expectation and silent judgment that Christians have let slip into our midst—that we're somehow the clean ones and everyone else is dirty. We may not say it to your face, but we'll reveal it in our actions, our looks, our body language and our silence. Once you clean yourself up and stop being such a sinner, then you are officially welcome to join our club and partake of our potlucks.

The story of Zacchaeus was always one of my favorites as a kid, but I never really got the point. I liked it because it felt humorous in a way, and any kind of humor that could be eked out of the Bible in those days was like water in a desert (everything always felt deadly serious regarding church and God).

> And when Jesus came to the place, He looked up and saw him, and said to him, "Zacchaeus, make haste and come down, for today I must stay at your house."
>
> Luke 19:5

I didn't get the point of the story, but I responded to the funny image of a really short guy having to climb a tree to see Jesus walking by. I used to think this was a story about our own effort. If we try hard enough and make ourselves stand out enough, then God will notice us and will reward us. But that's not what this is about at all.

Zacchaeus was a tax collector, which apparently was a really bad job to have amongst the Israelites because everyone knew you were a crook. The tax collectors always asked for more tax money than was necessary, and they would then skim off the top to glean more profits. It was kind of like legal mob activity. You had to pay or else; you knew you were being extorted.

Luke 19:2 tells us that Zacchaeus was rich, and it doesn't take a rocket scientist to realize why he was so rich. He had probably been a tax collector for quite some time, and he had been dishonest in his collection quite a bit. He had become rich off the backs of honest workers. Even in today's society this guy would be hated. Imagine if we all had IRS caseworkers assigned to take our taxes personally, and we all knew our caseworkers were making us pay more than we needed to pay. I'd want to punch that person in the mouth every time I saw him.

But on this day, Jesus was coming through town and the word had gotten out. One would *think* that Zacchaeus would have run to his home and hidden for fear of being called out as a royal-class sinner by this, the new leader of the moral revolution, but instead he did the opposite. In fact, if you read the gospels, you realize that sinners of all shapes and sizes tended to gravitate toward Jesus, and He thoroughly enjoyed their company. Even here, Zacchaeus didn't invite Jesus to his home. Jesus invited *Himself* to Zacchaeus' house! Jesus wanted to hang out with this guy.

What is going on here? Why are sinners so drawn to Jesus? Shouldn't they be ashamed of their sin, and, therefore, shouldn't they be trying to avoid Him? The fact that the opposite is always the case in the gospels should be a major tip-off to us of God's character as well as His nature.

The truth is, God is irresistible. Anyone who actually meets Him can't help but fall in love with Him. Unfortunately, the Church is quite resistible. There is a disconnect between the love Jesus shows and the love the Church shows. One of the places we filmed for *Furious Love* was a famous witchcraft and occult festival on the East Coast. We talked to a number of practicing witches and occultists, and what I learned was very, very interesting. Nearly all the people we talked to admitted that they had no issues with Jesus. They actually thought He was pretty cool. It was the Church that they hated, and Christians in particular.

As we dug deeper, we learned that many of these people had once belonged to a church. All of them had in some way been burned or abused by someone claiming to be a Christian, or they had simply grown sick and tired of the hypocrisy they saw every day. They were looking for something real, something they could control, and the occult appealed to them because it offered them power that came from "within themselves." Jesus was fine, but if a relationship with Him meant having to join this club full of hypocritical, angry, judgmental people, then they would have to decline that invitation.

Christians are known to get behind a myriad of "causes." Whether it's the anti-gay-marriage cause, the anti-abortion cause, or the "we need prayer in schools" cause, we tend to latch on to things that we think are important—things that we believe the rest of the world needs to agree with us about. At the risk of offending everyone who is reading this book, I would like to make the case that Jesus, our primary example for all things, was never interested in causes. He was always interested in people. In fact, that's pretty much all He seemed interested in. Just look at the episode with Zacchaeus as an example.

Zacchaeus is a short, dishonest man with a bit of a Napoleonic complex. He probably became a tax collector because he always had issues with his stature, and this job allowed him to have some power over the very people who too often rejected and made fun of him. He has made a ton of money through dishonest means, and he is probably only friends with other tax collectors and dishonest businessmen.

But for some reason, when he hears that Jesus is coming by, he desperately wants to catch a glimpse of Him. Why? What draws Zacchaeus to Jesus? I suppose it is the same thing that draws any sinner to Jesus. And that thing seems to be the one thing much of the Church has completely forgotten about when dealing with the outside world.

Jesus is God, and God is love. Therefore, Jesus is love. And by love, I mean love personified, in all its forms and permutations. When people encounter love, their entire beings shift. Their perspectives of life change. Their insides rumble with pleasure. They forget who they are. Their primary focus becomes the love they currently feel. This is because we have been made in the very image and likeness of God (remember Genesis?), and we have been created for love. To give and to receive it. Encountering the true love of God, then, ignites something within all of us because it, in a sense, completes us.

Zacchaeus is no different from anyone else who ever lived. He may have made a lot of bad decisions, but he has been created for love; it should really come as no surprise that something inside him leaps for joy when he hears that Jesus is near. So he lines up with the rest of the crowd, curses his shortness and then looks around for a better vantage point. There is something about this man, he senses, that is different.

He is drawn to the name or the reputation or the aura of Jesus. We don't know for sure what it is that fuels Zacchaeus' fervor to catch a glimpse of the Master, but whatever it is, he is not going to give up easily. He spots a sycamore tree (these are fairly low to the ground and can be climbed easily) and jumps onto it so he can get a better view of Jesus. I wonder if he is surrounded by children up there?

Jesus walks by and sees this little man in a tree. *What does He think?* I wonder. Is the Father speaking to Him right then, telling Him to go to that man's house for dinner? Does He laugh at the scene? Does He stop in shock and mutter "What the . . . ?" Who knows.

What we do know is that He calls out to Zacchaeus by name. He invites Himself over to this man's house, and He tells him to "make haste."

Jesus, as always, reveals the heart of the Father. He doesn't wait for sinners to get cleaned up and come to Him; He instead goes to them! He eats with them, parties with them and doesn't treat them like projects. He knows them by name. He knows all of us by name. He is the pursuer, not the pursued.

And what of the "make haste" comment? It feels a little out of place here. A normal conversation would go like this: "Hey, Zacchaeus, come on down from there, I'd like to eat dinner with you tonight." But Jesus tells him, in effect, to hurry up. Why?

This reveals one of the most wonderful aspects of the Father's heart that I have encountered in my six years of chasing after Him. Jesus doesn't tell Zacchaeus to hurry up because Zacchaeus needs to change his ways quickly. He tells Zacchaeus to hurry up because *He* can't wait to start a relationship with him.

There are two competing pictures of God, and one of them is held by most people. The first, most accepted picture, is that of God sitting on a cloud, distant, orchestrating everything, somewhat clinical, fairly unapproachable, definitely intimidating and a little grumpy. But Jesus, remember, reveals the heart of the Father, and here the heart of God is shown in full glory. Far from someone distant who is waiting for us to "get our heads straight" and make the long trek to His throne for mercy, God is instead pictured as a very, very eager Father, waiting anxiously for the go-ahead to invade our lives with love. "Make haste" is God's way of saying, "I've been waiting long enough for your friendship, and I don't want to wait any longer!"

Zacchaeus does make haste, and Jesus does go to his house, and a friendship begins. And the religious people of the day, the ones who have it all together and have cleaned themselves up in their own minds, are appalled that Jesus would choose to be friends with a notorious criminal with ties to the mob. Doesn't He worry about how this will look? About His reputation? Aren't these kinds of people the very reason we have causes—to stop them from doing what they do?

Perhaps the most telling aspect of this entire story is not what Jesus does, but what He doesn't do. We get no indication that Jesus tells Zacchaeus to stop being such a jerk and to stop his illegal activity. Just by meeting and spending time with Jesus, and as a result of His friendship, Zacchaeus stands up and declares that he's going to give half of his wealth to the poor, and if he has wronged people financially (which we know he has) he is going to restore their money to them fourfold!

What is going on here? While the religious folks stand on the outside furrowing their brows and judging the company

Jesus is keeping, the sheer presence and friendship of Jesus has such an effect on this "sinner" that he goes above and beyond what anyone could ever have dreamed for him regarding repentance and redemption.

Too often, it seems, the Church (and I'm at the front of this line, believe me) thinks that it is our job to change the minds and hearts of people. So we create programs or small groups or causes that are designed to educate people in the right thing to do, in the moral thing to do. By sheer force of will we hope people will change. We want them to change because, you know, it's the right thing to do. Because God hates sin. So you better stop sinning before it's too late.

But the problem with this approach is that too often it is not predicated on giving people their own interaction, their own relationship, their own *friendship* with Jesus. We preach principles when we should be preaching friendship. When you truly meet and befriend Jesus, you can't help but want to change. You don't want to change because it's the right thing to do, you want to change because it is what He wants. As is the case with all love affairs, when you truly love someone you care more about his or her desires and happiness than you do your own.

The reason so many Christians get such a bad rap from the world around us, it seems to me, is because we are more interested in changing behavior than introducing a Friend. Behavior is simply an outward expression of our inner desires, of what dominates our hearts. To try and change behavior without first encountering Jesus is not only useless, but often damaging as well. God is calling all of humanity to "make haste" and forge a friendship with Him.

The Loner

When I used to read through the gospels, I always pictured Jesus as a kind of roaming rock star, a social butterfly who oozed charisma and wanted to be surrounded by people all the time. But then I started noticing verses like the ones below, and I started to realize that He was human just like me, and He got sick of large crowds of people just like me, and He wanted to often be alone, just like me.

> Now in the morning, having risen a long while before daylight, He went out and departed to a solitary place; and there He prayed.
>
> Mark 1:35

> And when He had sent them away, He departed to the mountain to pray.
>
> Mark 6:46

> Now when it was day, He departed and went into a deserted place.
>
> Luke 4:42

> So He Himself often withdrew into the wilderness and prayed.
>
> Luke 5:16

> Now it came to pass in those days that He went out to the mountain to pray, and continued all night in prayer to God.
>
> Luke 6:12

Jesus, apparently, often sent His disciples away so He could have some alone time with the Father.

Why is this important?

Honestly, I don't want to worship a rock star. On the one hand, I think Jesus is modeling for us what a relationship with the Father should look like—it's a one-on-one marriage that requires quality time and attention. But looking at this another way, I think it reveals an important and wonderful part of God's personality. Jesus just wants to be alone once in a while. And a God who doesn't mind being alone is a God who, somehow, seems more personal and approachable to me.

I see in Jesus' desire to be alone a distinct, definite personality—one that has desires, likes and dislikes and real feelings. Another example of this is found in Genesis, when God admitted that on the seventh day of creation, He wanted to rest. Creating the entire universe wasn't effortless, apparently, even for God. This creation of His is so vast, so complex and so mind-boggling, that He pushed Himself and His own intelligence so hard that He felt the need to take a break afterward.

Growing up in church, I always fell into the trap of making God a faceless, emotionless ball of light that used worship to feed Itself. He was always "out there" somewhere, a kind of Other, and since He was so limitless and vast, there was no possible way I could relate to Him. So I focused on Jesus (well, the parts I wanted to focus on) and let the Father kind of fall by the wayside.

But the God of the Bible, the God who walks with us and desires friendship with us, is an actual Person. He can actually stand somewhere (see Moses), He can walk around with us (see Adam and Eve), He can take a rest (see Creation) and He can have friends (keep reading).

A Penchant for the Dramatic

The story of Lazarus being raised from the dead always intrigued me—mostly because of the peculiar things contained within the story that made absolutely no sense to me. It is a dramatic story with a vivid sense of time and place, which is probably why I always liked it so much. But something bubbles beneath the surface of this story that cannot, and must not, be ignored.

Jesus was good friends with Lazarus, who was the brother of Mary and Martha. The Bible tells us that Jesus "loved" Lazarus, so we know they were more than acquaintances. This was a family Jesus cared for deeply. They also had deep faith in Him, as became evident when both sisters told Jesus separately that if only He had gotten there sooner, their brother would be alive today. Obviously Lazarus was a sick man at the end, and the sisters both believed that Jesus not only could have but would have healed their brother had He arrived a few days earlier. Yet even they had their limits as far as what they believed He could do.

The first strange thing I notice about this story is perhaps the most obvious. Jesus gets word that His good friend is deathly ill, yet He decides to stay put for a few more days instead of heading out immediately. The most obvious reasoning for this is that the Father has already briefed Him on the plan, and He is simply allowing time for His friend to die. A resurrection from the dead is put on the schedule. .

Once again, most of us who have read or heard this story over and over again simply breeze by with the full knowledge of what our Lord is up to. We kind of chuckle to ourselves that we're "in" on the whole thing. Jesus makes a few vague

218

statements to His disciples about what's about to go down, but they, true to form, don't understand a word of it. But we, the audience, knowing the outcome, place the patina of inevitability over this story and fail to explore its strangeness.

Jesus knows full well that He is supposed to go raise Lazarus from the dead, so He waits around until He's pretty sure the guy is good and gone. I always used to look at this story from Jesus' perspective, since He is the main focus. But then, as I began exploring the friendship aspect of this episode, I began to think about poor Lazarus. You can assume that since he is sick enough for his sisters to send a message to Jesus (it's not like they had email), the guy was suffering quite a bit. This is Jesus' very, very good friend, a man He loves dearly, and he is suffering, we assume, quite horribly. Jesus can show up anytime and relieve him of his suffering—and, in fact, that's exactly what the plan is . . . for the most part. Yet the poor guy is left to suffer until the throes of death finally take him for good.

Why? Jesus makes it good and clear for us: "This sickness is not unto death, but for the glory of God, that the Son of God may be glorified through it" (John 11:4).

See this for what it plainly is, and I hope understanding begins to dawn on you. Lazarus is sick—such a simple word and concept, yet if you are so sick that you are about to die, you know that it is not a fun place to be. In fact, it's about as horrible as things get. And the sole purpose of this sickness is that "the Son of God may be glorified through it."

I have heard my fair share of sermons touting the fact that the perfect will of God is for us to be healthy, happy and prosperous. While I agree for the most part with this assessment (what father *doesn't* want good things for his children?), I also cannot escape this story, among countless others in the Bible, where very good friends of God are forced to endure incredible hardships for "the ultimate glory of God."

There are some who may read this and be disgusted. If I let pain afflict my children, even though I have the ability to relieve them of their pain anytime I want, and I wait to do so until the precise moment that I will receive the most glory for it, there will be ample grounds not only to relieve me of my parental duties, but also to throw me into jail! So why is God allowed to do it this way? How can we rectify something like this story with His statement: "Every good gift and every perfect gift is from above, and comes down from the Father of lights" (James 1:17)?

There are two reasons, I think, and I'll mention the lesser one first.

God, it seems, has a penchant for the dramatic.

Read almost any story in the Bible and you'll see it, plain as day. Noah is putting animals in the ark just as the rain begins. Moses must wait until the people are about to riot against him before God brings water from a rock. Abraham has raised the knife to kill his son, and only then does God stop him. And it goes on and on, story after story. Events are allowed to unfold until they reach such a point that all seems lost, and that is when God steps in and does His God stuff.

Or look at your own life. Have you ever wondered why God always seems to wait until the last minute to touch your life? Your house payment is due tomorrow morning, and you hear a knock at your door this evening from someone bringing you a check. You have a great need for something and then, just before you must have it, something happens that fulfills your need. We have all experienced or heard stories like this, and I've always wondered why God does it that way. Why not give me what I need, like, a week before I need it? Why not save me the stress?

Need a few more examples? Jesus, perhaps more than anyone in the Bible, practically screams bold, dramatic action. Remember when He walks on the water? The disciples are in their boat, struggling to get to shore, and it's the middle of the night. Jesus sees them there, and for whatever reason (time, probably), He decides to walk on top of the water to catch up and get to their destination on time. But He doesn't *have* to walk so near their boat that they see Him. He could have bypassed them a little farther away, slipping by them and giving them all a good startle when they arrive at port the next morning. But instead He makes sure He's close enough for them to see Him.

Or after His resurrection, when the disciples have gathered together in Galilee because He told them to, He walks through a wall, scaring the living daylights out of them. He isn't a ghost, but is indeed solid flesh (as evidenced by His eating some fish and letting them touch His body). Which means He could just as easily use the doorknob. But that's no way for a resurrected man to make an appearance! Let's do the walk-through-the-wall trick instead.

Or what about His telling Peter to go fishing, open the mouth of the first fish he catches and pull a coin out of the fish's mouth so they can pay the tax that is due? Are you kidding me? There's not an easier, less elaborate way to get a coin than this?

The examples could go on and on. The point, of course, is that Jesus is not your average boring "churchy" guy. He's creative, a tad mischievous, quite funny and likes to make an impression.

While this may indeed simply be His personality, my guess is there is more to it than just that. And the second reason is the real gripper.

God, as we have seen, is a storyteller, and the dramatic runs in all storytellers' blood. It's the best way to get the audience's attention, to keep them riveted, to keep them interested. And isn't that ultimately God's greatest desire? He is shackled by an invisibility cloak so that true love might exist, and He must, therefore, work most effectively while remaining invisible. And any storyteller worth his salt knows that to make the best impact, you need to set up situations that are going to grip and ultimately wow the audience.

God wants to get our attention, plain and simple. We, with our fickle hearts and halfhearted love, care mostly about ourselves. When we get into trouble, our main concern is ourselves, and how we can get ourselves out of trouble. So we turn to the all-powerful God to get us out of a jam. His main concern is quite a bit different from ours. He is wholly devoted to our hearts and our eternal friendship and relationship with Him, and while He certainly does care about our immediate needs, He always takes the long view of things.

Herein lies the main difference between our feeble little brains and His Almighty Cranium. For us, the long view is a few years. For Him, it is eternity. He understands our existence beyond this world, and our relationship with Him will continue forever in heaven. But we can barely see past our own noses, our own sicknesses and our own problems. We are so consumed with the here and now that we cannot comprehend the there and then of God.

So we blame Him for everything. He's not coming back fast enough. He's allowing too much bad stuff to happen in the world. He's not taking my cancer away. He's not healing my back. He's not this. He's not that. If only He would show up in time, then all this pain and heartache would be over. If only He had shown up a few days earlier, Lazarus would never have died.

Yet here Jesus clearly has other intentions. He tells His disciples, after waiting a few days, that they are heading back to Judea. It is finally time to go see Lazarus. The disciples think this is a terrible idea, because they know the Jews there tried to stone Him to death the last time. Jesus answers them with a cryptic statement:

> "Are there not twelve hours in the day? If anyone walks in the day, he does not stumble, because he sees the light of this world. But if one walks in the night, he stumbles, because the light is not in him."
>
> John 11:9–10

What the heck is He talking about? The disciples ask Him a simple question, and He gives them this? Sometimes it's not easy being a disciple of Jesus. He's always the smartest guy in the room. You can't hold a candle to Him. But we know the full story, so what does this mean?

Jesus fully understands the situation when He makes this statement. His disciples don't understand the logic of Jesus' delay and then His decision to go, but Jesus is operating under

223

the logic of God, which is radically different, wildly creative and concerned with the whole *as well as* the individual. Jesus' words about walking in the light as opposed to walking in the darkness should be clear enough to us. He is the light; His understanding of things is fully illuminated. Our fleshly understanding of situations is shrouded in the darkness of our finite minds.

A true friend trusts completely. Many times, when I do not understand something my friends are preparing to do on my behalf, rather than waste time explaining they simply say, "Just trust me," and get on with it. At the end of the day, if we truly want to be friends with God and to receive the fullness of that friendship, we have to come to a place where we can simply say, "Okay, God. I don't get it, and in many respects I don't even agree with it, but I trust You."

I am certain that Lazarus trusted that his good friend would show up, once He was sent for, and restore him to health. This much is implied by the fact that both of his sisters came to Jesus with a hint of accusation in their statements that "if only You had come sooner." You have to wonder if Mary and Martha heard Lazarus' rasping voice on his deathbed, wondering aloud where in the world Jesus was. Why wasn't He coming? I thought we were better friends than this? I wonder if, as he drew his last painful breath, Lazarus felt a stab of betrayal at his Friend's lack of concern. Certainly Mary and Martha both felt it.

Yet Jesus had other, greater things in mind for Lazarus. As a result of this event, John 11:45 tells us that "many of the Jews who had come to Mary, and had seen the things Jesus did, believed in Him." More were added to the Kingdom.

More hearts were restored to the Father. More of the devil's ground was taken back.

Was it worth it? I suppose it depends on whom you ask. Ask Mary, Martha and Lazarus, who had to endure all the pain and hardship, and they probably say yes, but maybe they hesitate a little before giving the right answer. Ask the people who believed, and therefore found eternal life, and I'm guessing you have far less hesitation.

As I write this, I live in America. We are a free nation, with liberties unprecedented in human history. When we read about Jesus saying, "Blessed are those who are persecuted for righteousness' sake, for theirs is the kingdom of heaven" (Matthew 5:10), we tend to apply that to others. We don't get persecuted much here. Our lives are not in danger for believing in Jesus. That's how I always viewed the "persecution" stuff in the Bible. I glossed over it because, well, I'm in no danger of being tortured for my faith.

But is persecution limited to physical torture? Could "persecution for righteousness' sake" possibly mean more than someone cutting or burning me? Could persecution sometimes be God taking longer than I want for Him to show up, thus causing me pain and heartache just so He can teach me something or reach someone else through whatever it is I am going through? I have heard countless stories, for example, of people getting saved by witnessing someone's death. They see how that person faced down death, how he or she never wavered in belief and trust in the goodness of God, and they are won over by the power of another person's radical love for an invisible God.

I know that God's perfect plan does not include sickness in the world, but, at the same time, we cannot all live forever.

We will all die of something. That is not to say that we don't contend and plead for Jesus to come before it is too late, but sometimes, it seems, He chooses, for reasons all His own, to arrive when it is too late.

But before you accuse Jesus of orchestrating your suffering for His own purposes (which is not the case here, by the way—Jesus didn't cause Lazarus to get sick), what Jesus does next proves that He is not a cold, clinical, heartless tyrant who cares only for His "Master Plan."

Honestly, that was the view I had of God for the longest time. He was like a giant computer, processing possibilities with variables and crunching the data, and whatever outcome led to the greatest profit for Him, that was what He allowed to happen. He wasn't personal; He was a God-machine.

Jesus, being the exact representation of the Father's heart, blows a hole through that theory by what comes next. This is the part of the story that made zero sense to me. Growing up, I attended a Lutheran school in my hometown of Monroe, Michigan, and whenever my friends and I were told we had to learn a Bible verse for some reason, some smart aleck in our group would inevitably bust out with the "Jesus wept" verse. It was a joke to us. The shortest verse in the Bible. It never made sense to me. What a weird verse! Not, "Jesus sat down and wept," or any other variation that would probably flow better. Just two words, sitting there, drawing attention to themselves. Why?

Go back into the scene, and it makes even less sense. Jesus knows Lazarus is dead, and He also knows that in a short time he's not going to be dead anymore. *He knows the whole deal!* Yet here He is, comforting Martha and Mary, making them take Him out to the tomb, and then He starts crying. Why is He crying? Doesn't He know that this is all about to change in, like, ten minutes?

John 11:32–33 is the key. Jesus is the picture of stoicism up until this point. He's cool, calm and collected; doesn't rush ahead of His emotions; patiently waits on the Father's signal. Martha, the practical, rational one, comes to Him and they have a normal conversation. Jesus even gives hints to her about what He's about to do, although she misses the point.

But then Mary shows up. The passionate, emotional one. She falls at the feet of Jesus, a total mess, a complete wreck. This is the moment everything changes. Verse 33 says, "Therefore, when Jesus saw her weeping, and the Jews who came with her weeping, He groaned in the spirit and was troubled." Shortly thereafter, Jesus wept.

These women are His friends. He knows this entire family personally and intimately. Even though He knows the ultimate outcome, even though He is fully aware that their pain will end, even though He knows that this had to take place "so that the Son of Man might be lifted up," He *still* gets broken over our brokenness. He cries with us. He does not stand aside, emotionless, waiting for our hysteria to abate so He can move forward with the Master Plan. He comes right to us, He joins us and He weeps with us.

If you want to know God's personality, it is on display for you in this story in brilliant colors. In fact, this moment, this tiny verse, the tiniest of verses in the entire Bible, says more about the God of the universe than perhaps anything else in the Bible.

Jesus wept.

What does it mean? It means that the God we serve is emotion through and through. Even though He understands the end game, sees everything for what it really is, our emotions affect His emotions. If I don't know you well, and I see you crying because of something that happened to you, I might feel some semblance of pity or sadness. If you are my best friend and I see you crying from a tragedy, I will weep with you because I care for you. Jesus doesn't cry in this story because He is sad that Lazarus is dead. Jesus cries because the family He loves is sad. Never mind that in a few minutes they won't be sad. God cares about us in the here and now. He is just that involved.

God is love. But too often we forget that with love come emotions. Whatever emotions we have for those we love, consider the magnitude of God's love, and then consider the magnitude of His emotions over every aspect of your life. He loves us way more than we can ever love Him, and, therefore, the shimmering radiance of His emotions over us is simply breathtaking.

In the end, everything about God's personality and character points to one thing: relationship. It's what His whole book points to and makes possible. It's why He entered His own story. And it's why He made you.

Friendship with God

This book you are holding is a book about friendship with God. It is about looking between, inside and around the stories of the Bible to try and find some clarity of God's character and nature. As I have already mentioned, we are in luck in this pursuit because we are not bound solely to stories from the Old Testament to do this; we have the living embodiment of the Father in the Person of Jesus Christ.

This next and final story that we are going to look at is one—I'm going to be honest here—that always freaked me out: the story of Jesus' Transfiguration.

> Now after six days Jesus took Peter, James, and John his brother, led them up on a high mountain by themselves; and He was transfigured before them. His face shone like the sun, and His clothes became as white as the light.
>
> Matthew 17:1–2

Sure, all throughout the gospels Jesus does high-level spiritual stuff, but at least He remains a fairly normal dude while He is doing it. But when He gets transfigured, He always seemed to me to go from being a normal dude with superpowers, to being, well, God.

It was always easier for me to think of Jesus as a normal guy, because I could relate to a normal guy. I was a normal guy. But when you started to move into God-man territory, that's when it began to feel more like church. And as I've admitted freely, I wasn't sure I fully trusted that God character. Jesus, absolutely. God, not so much.

So when the lines started to blur, as they do in this story, I didn't know what to do with it. God was wholly "other," whereas Jesus was here and now. The whole Trinity thing just wigged me out completely. It made my brain want to explode trying to understand it. Yet even here, in this Transfiguration story, I found ways to twist things to further my own belief that I was a second-class citizen in God's eyes. Even when He displayed His love for His Son—this, ultimately, is the very heart of the Father—I always spun my thinking toward, *Well, yeah, of course He loves Jesus. Who* doesn't *love Jesus? He's perfect!* And then I was reminded that I was very much not perfect, was in fact kind of a jerk, and sank further into my stupor of believing that God probably wasn't super happy with me.

Needless to say, a lot has changed in my personal theology since then. And even though this story has some pretty big special effects going on, that's not my main focus here. I'm more interested in looking at something that I never saw until recently.

The story goes like this. Jesus heads up a mountain with "the big three" of the disciples, and while they're up there, Jesus gets lit up, Holy Spirit–style, and His face shines like the sun and His clothes become whiter than bleach. Then, suddenly, Moses and Elijah show up and start talking to Jesus; the gang is back together again. And that's when Peter (thank God for Peter; he makes me feel so much better about myself) blurts out something about building tents for the guys.

At this point (and I just love this), God writes: "While he [Peter] was still speaking, behold, a bright cloud overshadowed them; and suddenly a voice came out of the cloud, saying, 'This is My beloved Son, in whom I am well pleased. Hear Him!'" (Matthew 17:5). God wouldn't include this little fact of *while he was still speaking* unless He has good reason for it to be in there. The meaning of the statement is obvious: God interrupts Peter. But the next question, I'm sure you know by now, has to be *Why?*

Why doesn't God just allow Peter to finish his stupid remark, then bust out His "beloved Son" speech? God is way too smart to do anything without cause or reason, so I was always curious as to why this tidbit is included in the story.

First off, I don't think it is to belittle Peter. That in itself would go against the very heart of God. It might be His way of showing Peter, in no uncertain terms, that that idea is incredibly misguided. Peter probably has good intentions. This could become a holy hotspot. They could sell kabobs and make a killing. Whatever His reasoning, God could be interrupting him to let him know, basically, to shut up.

But I wonder if something else is going on here. Look at what God's speech is about: how much He loves His Son; how pleased He is with His Son. You almost get the impression that the Father is looking longingly at His Son, in whom He delights so much, and He just can't help Himself any longer. Even while Peter is speaking, the Father's love bursts out of Him, flooding everyone present. He's not being rude; He's simply so filled with love and passion for His kid that He has to say so and can't possibly wait a minute more. We saw what happened to Moses when he didn't circumcise his own son and in a sense got in the way of the Father's plan for His Son. We would do well to remember here that, at this point, the Father has eyes only for His Son, and it breaks forth on the Mountain of Transfiguration.

But let us leave that moment alone and move to another aspect of this story that I find so intriguing and remarkable. Six days prior to this, Jesus admonished Peter to "get behind Me, Satan" when Peter complained that Jesus shouldn't die. Peter has shown complete lack of understanding of the mission of his Master. Yet here he is, on the Mountain of Transfiguration, an eyewitness to one of the most startling events in the Bible. Why is this guy—who brings me such joy because he's such a numbskull—even here?

Jesus knows what He is doing and where He is going when He sets off up the mountain. And He presumably tells nine other disciples to hang back while He takes the big three up the mountain with Him. I always noticed this as a kid—that Jesus always seems to take Peter, James and John with Him when He does the super crazy stuff—but I never gave it much thought. Then, as I began to learn more about the heart and character of God, it finally dawned on me. Jesus brings these guys with Him for one reason, and one reason only.

They are His best friends.

Just about everywhere Jesus goes, He brings all of His disciples with Him. But for this historic moment, a moment that will define who He is, He chooses to bring only three guys with Him. For such an important occasion, Jesus wants only His closest friends with Him.

Think of your own big moments in life. Your wedding day. Your child's birth. Your birthday. Shoot, even when you get those amazing free tickets for once in your life. On those occasions, what do you want more than anything? To share this moment with the ones who are closest to you. You don't invite an acquaintance to that big game; you invite your best bud. The big, important things in life are that much bigger and more important when you can share them with the people you like the most. Jesus was no different.

Yet, of course, this begs a new question, doesn't it? If Jesus had different levels of friendship with His disciples (which I don't think it too farfetched to think), then might He have different levels of friendship with us? Might He be better friends with some of us than He is with others? Keep in mind I am not talking about love here. Love and friendship are two very different things. God loves all of us equally, because we are all His children. But throughout His entire story He has been creating, He has made it perfectly clear that some people are just closer friends to Him than others are.

I don't think this has as much to do with God looking around and saying, "Hmm, I like his personality. I choose him," as it is us saying, "Yes, Lord, I'll do whatever it takes to be Your friend. How can I bless You?" God has also shown throughout His story that He often chooses the most unlikely people in the world as His close friends. Obviously He sees something in their hearts that He is drawn to—something that tells Him this person will respond to Him in a way others won't.

Love is a gift, yet friendship, which is brought about by trust, must be earned. In Jesus' darkest hour in the Garden of Gethsemane, Jesus wasn't brokenhearted because He was about to be killed. (He was greatly stressed by that, but that is not what broke His heart.) He was brokenhearted because His supposed friends, His best friends, cared more about sleep than they did Him.

Yet His love for His friends was unquenchable. Even Judas Iscariot, who the Lord knew would betray Him, was given a place of honor at the Last Supper. Jesus would remain His friend, would keep loving and honoring this scoundrel to the very last.

Take one, final look at this scene. This time, though, enter it through the eyes of Peter, James and John. These are Jesus' best friends, and you just know they're feeling pretty good that they were chosen while the other saps are left behind at the base of the mountain.

But then, Peter doesn't get what's going on, gets interrupted by God, and all three of them are on their faces, more terrified than they've ever been in their lives. They are surrounded by the glory cloud of God; His voice is booming in their ears; Jesus is lit up like a Christmas tree; Moses and Elijah are presumably back from the dead. These three bumpkins are no match for everything that is happening in this scene, and they resort to falling on their faces and freaking out.

Keep in mind, this is what friendship with Jesus looks like. Acquaintances stay down at the base of the mountain and can see that something is happening up there, but true friends of God, His best friends, are in the thick of it, and *it* is usually far more than they ever imagined or can even bear. Jesus may seem like a regular dude, but He's far from it. He's the most wonderful, terrifying Person in the universe. You become His friend at your own risk.

But it's the best risk you will ever take.

Darren Wilson is the founder of Wanderlust Productions, a film/television production company in Chicago that focuses on creating media that creatively and powerfully advances the Kingdom of God around the world. He created the non-profit Wanderlust Foundation, which is dedicated to bringing hope, dignity and a voice to the voiceless. Before turning to full-time production work, he taught for thirteen years at Judson University in Elgin, Illinois. Darren was recently named one of the 21 Emerging Leaders of Tomorrow's Church by *Charisma* magazine. Darren lives with his wife, Jenell, and their three children, Serenity, Stryder and River, in the Chicago area.

Darren's films have been seen by millions around the world. His first three films, *Finger of God*, *Furious Love* and *Father of Lights*, have together sold more than 200,000 copies almost entirely through word-of-mouth. Darren's first book, *Filming God*, details his incredible journey from skeptic to believer in the miraculous.

For more information on Darren and what he and Wanderlust Productions are currently working on, visit: www.wpfilm.com, or follow him on Facebook, Twitter or Instagram.

Don't get stuck at asking "What would Jesus do"— be equipped to *do* it.

Chicagoland pastor Robby Dawkins hadn't moved past that question either—until he discovered that the miraculous things Jesus did during His lifetime are not just history. They are today's reality. When he started living the way Jesus did, he started living a life, as he says, straight out of a superhero movie.

So can you. In this dangerous book, you'll learn simple, practical ways to take hold of your God-given "power tools"—prophetic ministry, healing, ministering the presence of God and deliverance from demonic power. And through amazing but true stories from the front lines of ministry, you'll see what happens when ordinary Christians harness God's superpower to bring His Kingdom to earth.

It's time to beat the sickness, suffering and despair of the impossible. It's time to embrace a powerful faith. **It's time to do what Jesus did.**

Do What Jesus Did by Robby Dawkins

✔Chosen